AF474024

I AM YOUR GOD

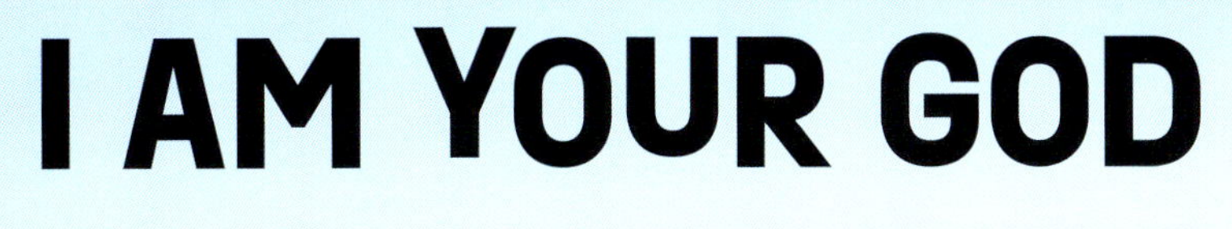

90 faith-building devotions

BEKAH GRACE

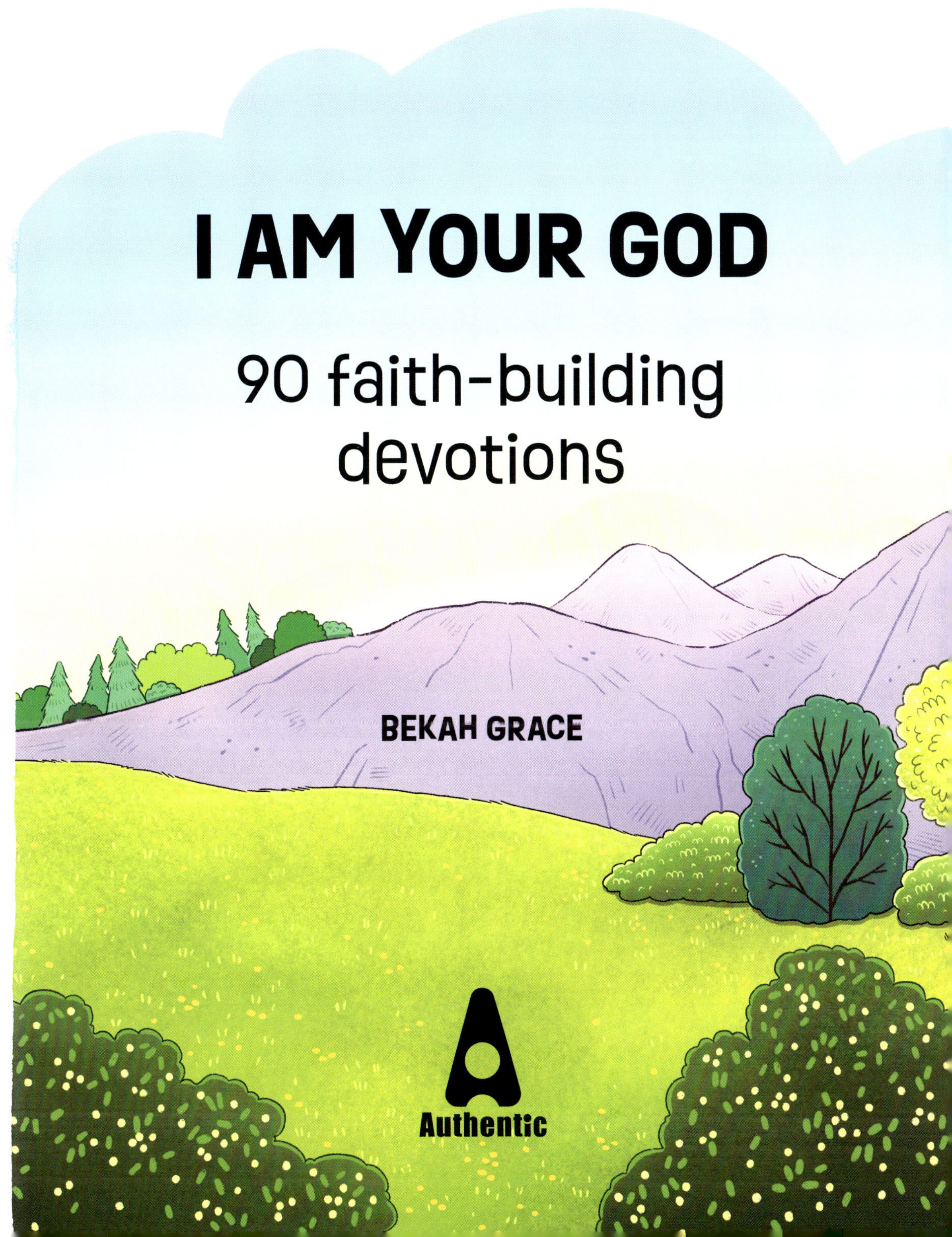

Authentic

31 30 29 28 27 26 25 7 6 5 4 3 2 1

First published 2025 by Authentic Media Limited,
PO Box 6326, Bletchley, Milton Keynes, MK1 9GG.
authenticmedia.co.uk

British Library Cataloguing in Publication Data
A catalogue record for this book is available from the British Library.
ISBN: 978-1-78893-350-6

Cover design by Bekah Grace
Printed and bound in China.

Dedication and Acknowledgements

For my good Shepherd, who is faithful even when I am not.

And to my friends, family, and sweet husband, I am deeply thankful for you. This book wouldn't be what it is today without you.

THIS BOOK IS PRESENTED TO:

BY:

ON:

CONTENTS

Dedication and Acknowledgements
Introduction
How to Use This Book
Introduction to God (the Trinity)
Day 1: I Am Your Father
Day 2: I Am Your Hope
Day 3: I Am Your Planner
Day 4: I Am Your Life
Day 5: I Am Your Good Shepherd
Day 6: I Am Your Provider
Day 7: I Am Your Saviour
Day 8: I Am Your Strength
Day 9: I Am Your Helper
Day 10: I Am Your Warrior
Day 11: I Am Your Rest
Day 12: I Am Your Reason
Day 13: I Am Your True Love
Day 14: I Am Your Life Preserver
Day 15: I Am Your Comforter
Day 16: I Am Your Judge

Day 17: I Am Your Rock

Day 18: I Am Your Friend

Day 19: I Am Your Gift Giver

Day 20: I Am Your Light

Day 21: I Am Your Creator

Day 22: I Am Your Eternal Refill

Day 23: I Am Your Redeemer

Day 24: I Am Your Foundation

Day 25: I Am Your Healer

Day 26: I Am Your King

Day 27: I Am Your Caregiver

Day 28: I Am Your Miracle Worker

Day 29: I Am Your Way Maker

Day 30: I Am Your Warm Embrace

Day 31: I Am Your Stain Remover

Day 32: I Am Your Confidence

Day 33: I Am Your Listening Ear

Day 34: I Am Your Restoration

Day 35: I Am Your Identity

Day 36: I Am Your Advocate

Day 37: I Am Your Shield

Day 38: I Am Your Anchor

Day 39: I Am Your Forgiveness

Day 40: I Am Your Brother

Day 41: I Am Your Solid Ground

Day 42: I Am Your Victory

Day 43: I Am Your Gardener

Day 44: I Am Your Master

Day 45: I Am Your Shelter

Day 46: I Am Your Instructor

Day 47: I Am Your Protector

Day 48: I Am Your Righteousness

Day 49: I Am Your Builder

Day 50: I Am Your Door

Day 51: I Am Your Encourager

Day 52: I Am Your Example

Day 53: I Am Your Promise Keeper

Day 54: I Am Your New Beginning

Day 55: I Am Your Hiding Place

Day 56: I Am Your Guide

Day 57: I Am Your High Priest

Day 58: I Am Your Faithful One

Day 59: I Am Your Freedom

Day 60: I Am Your Strong Tower

Day 61: I Am Your Constant

Day 62: I Am Your Counsellor

Day 63: I Am Your Authority

Day 64: I Am Your Breath of Life

Day 65: I Am Your Inspiration

Day 66: I Am Your Shoulder to Cry On

Day 67: I Am Your Safe Place

Day 68: I Am Your Treasure

Day 69: I Am Your Justice

Day 70: I Am Your Mediator

Day 71: I Am Your Joy

Day 72: I Am Your Guardian

Day 73: I Am Your Good News

Day 74: I Am Your Equipper

Day 75: I Am Your Captain

Day 76: I Am Your Companion

Day 77: I Am Your Home

Day 78: I Am Your Voice of Truth

Day 79: I Am Your Power

Day 80: I Am Your Potter

Day 81: I Am Your Vine

Day 82: I Am Your Armour

Day 83: I Am Your Bread

Day 84: I Am Your Avenger

Day 85: I Am Your Second Chance

Day 86: I Am Your Rescuer

Day 87: I Am Your Teacher

Day 88: I Am Your Ally

Day 89: I Am Your Beginning and End

Day 90: I Am Your Peace

Conclusion: I AM WHO I AM

INTRODUCTION

This book is filled with daily reminders of who God is and how he interacts with us in our daily lives!

Throughout the next ninety days you will get the chance to explore several aspects of God's character and personhood.

Although there are many more titles we could give God, I hope and pray you will find joy in the titles written about in this book.

May you enjoy seeing God for the beautiful friend he is and for all he does in your life EVERY DAY!

Let's pray.

Dear God, thank you for your unconditional love for me. I want to have a personal relationship with you and get to know you better every day. Please inspire me to read my Bible, pray and spend time with you so that our friendship grows deeper. I trust that you will show yourself to me as I learn more about you.

HOW TO USE THIS BOOK

This book is written in ninety parts, one part each day for ninety days! Each part includes a statement about God, for example: 'I am your Father.' Along with each statement there is a Bible verse, a short explanation, some questions and a prayer!

Over the next ninety days you'll be able to explore who God says he is through the Bible. And by learning who God is, you will start to notice ways to connect with and talk to God throughout every life experience.

Each day be prepared to explore a new aspect of God's person. Make time to read the Bible verse, think about the questions and talk to God in prayer.

I encourage you to discuss the questions with a family member or trusted friend. The questions will help you explore the thoughts and feelings you have in your head and heart.

You may or may not already know a bit about who God is and what he does. However, regardless of how much you already know about him, God is infinite! We will never know everything about him or everything he does.

So, I encourage you to see these ninety devotionals as a chance to see God in a new way every day. And to appreciate him for his constant involvement in your life.

I believe these next ninety days will give you many reasons to want to grow in your relationship with God and love him more.

INTRODUCTION TO GOD (THE TRINITY)

Throughout this book you will see three characters which represent God.

The God of the Bible, the God who created heaven and earth is ONE God. But there are three persons in God, God the Father, God the son (Jesus), and God the Holy Spirit.

We call the unity of these three persons in ONE God, the Trinity.

So, although you see the three persons of God represented through the illustrations, we have only ONE God.

It is tricky to understand – even adults who have known God a long time find it tricky!

If you have questions, or want to learn more, I encourage you to ask your questions, read more books, and talk to other Christians!

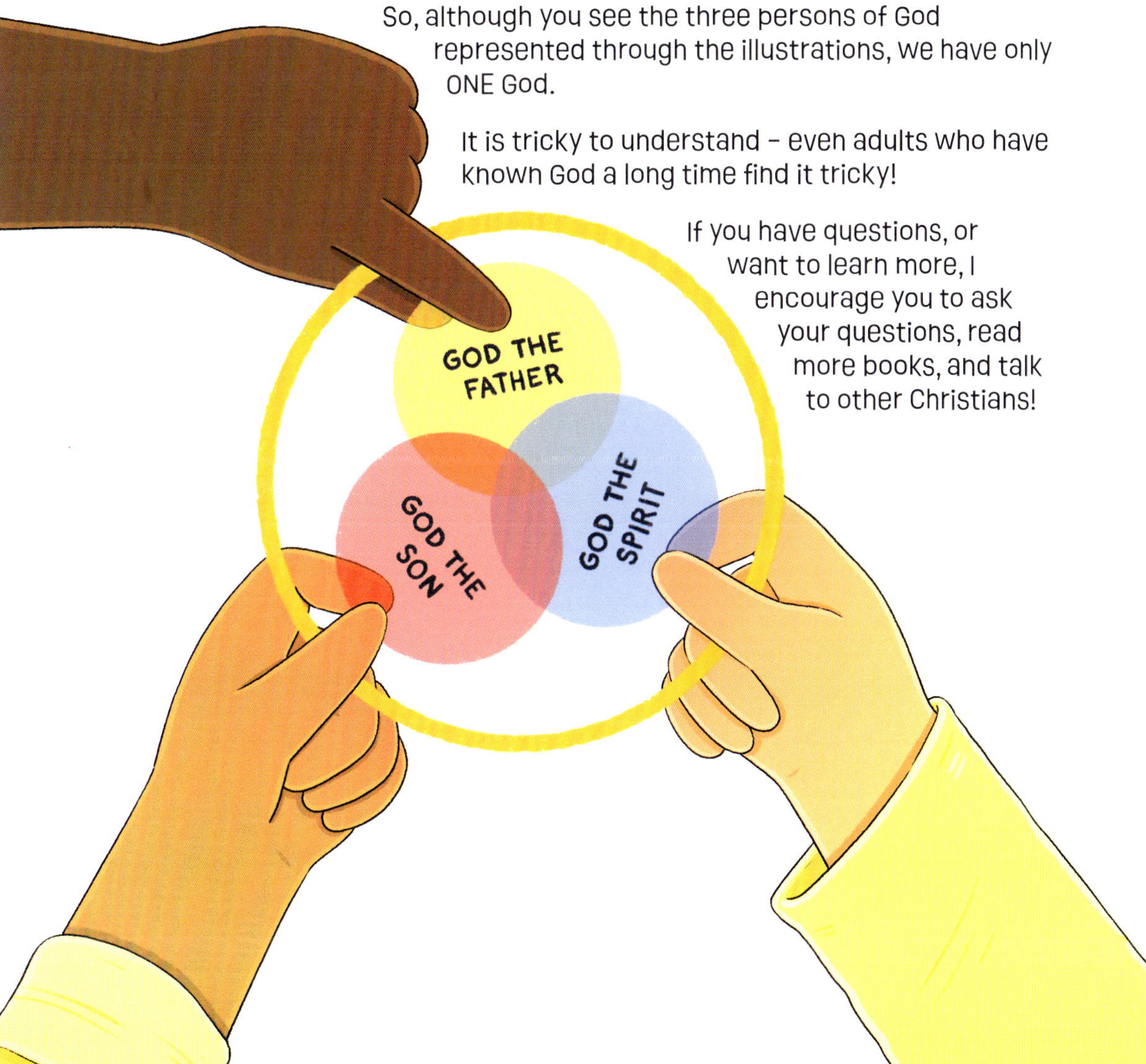

Introduction to God the Father

Hello! I'm the Father. The maker of the universe and your creator. When the people I created disobeyed me, I created a plan to win them back, forgive their sins, and set them free from sin and death! I love the world so much, that I sent my only Son to earth to die and save my creation.

(John 3:16) (Genesis 1:1) (John 6:38)

Introduction to God the Son/Jesus

Hi, I'm the Son of God, Jesus. I was born to the virgin Mary so I could live life on earth and give my life as a sacrifice to save the world from sin and death. I was crucified, buried, and raised to life on the third day! Now I sit at the right hand of God the Father in heaven.

(John 3:16) (Matthew 1:18-25) (Matthew 27)
(1 Corinthians 15:55-57) (Hebrews 10:12)

Introduction to God the Holy Spirit

Hey, I'm the Holy Spirit. I was sent by Jesus to be with his followers, also called 'believers', after he went back to heaven. I remind believers of Jesus' words, fill them with strength, and help them live a life pleasing to God. I live inside Jesus' followers and give them peace, hope, and love. I go wherever they go, giving them gifts and power to serve God.

(John 16:7) (John 14:16-17)
(1 Corinthians 6:19)
(Acts 1:8) (John 14:26)

I AM YOUR FATHER

When birds are sold, two small birds cost only a penny. But not even one of the little birds can die without your Father's knowing it. God even knows how many hairs are on your head. So don't be afraid. You are worth much more than many birds.

Matthew 10:29-31

God is our Father, and we are his children. He knows every detail about us. He even knows the number of hairs on our head! Are we more valuable than a bird? YES, God says we are!

If God takes care of even the tiniest bird, he will definitely take care of his own children. So, we don't need to be afraid of anything because God will take care of us.

Whenever we see a small bird, we can remember that our heavenly Father sees us and is taking care of us.

QUESTION TIME!

How many birds do you think you're worth?

How does God know so much about you (even the number of hairs on your head!!)?

What makes God a good father?

How does it make you feel to know you're a child of God?

LET'S PRAY . . .

Dear God, thank you that you see me as valuable, and that you take care of me. You are a good father and I love you.
Amen.

I AM YOUR HOPE

We were made right with God by His grace. And God gave us the Spirit so that we could receive the life that never ends. That is what we hope for.

Titus 3:7

Sometimes we talk about 'hoping' certain things will happen. For example, 'hoping' we do well on our maths test or 'hoping' our football team wins the match. But what does it mean for God to be OUR hope?

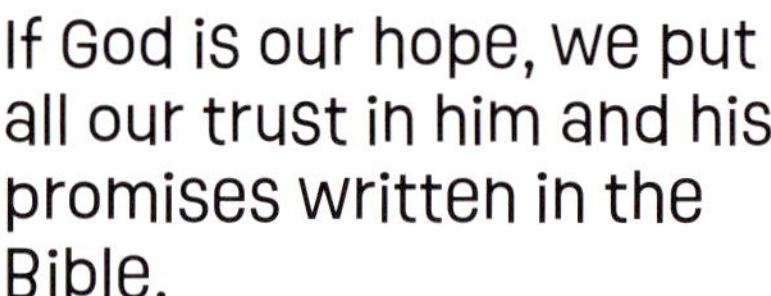

If God is our hope, we put all our trust in him and his promises written in the Bible.

No matter what happens in life, if God is our hope, we know that one day there will be no more evil and we will live with God in heaven forever. In God, our hope is a reality, not just a wish.

QUESTION TIME!

Have you ever hoped for something that didn't happen?

Can you imagine a world with no more evil? What would it be like?

Why can you trust God to be your hope?

What things can you look forward to because God is your hope?

LET'S PRAY . . .

Dear God, thank you for giving me your grace so that I can put all my hope in you. When my hope is in you, I have a lot to look forward to!

Amen.

3

I AM YOUR PLANNER

'I say this because I know what I have planned for you,' says the Lord. 'I have good plans for you. I don't plan to hurt you. I plan to give you hope and a good future.

Jeremiah 29:11

We all make plans for our lives. We plan what to wear in the morning and what games to play with our friends. Did you know God makes plans for our lives too?

The God who created the earth and put the stars in the sky cares enough about our lives to make plans for us! He says his plans are to give us hope and a GOOD future.

Even when things aren't going the way we want them to, we have a God who has a good plan for us. Just imagine all the wonderful things God has planned for each one of our futures! We can trust his plan.

QUESTION TIME!

What plans do you have for today?

Can you name some things you hope for in the future?

Do you ever ask God what his plans are for you each day?

What kinds of good plans do you think God has in store for you?

LET'S PRAY . . .

Dear God, thank you that you have lots of good plans for me! I will trust you to give me hope and a good future.
Amen.

I AM YOUR LIFE

God wanted them to look for him and perhaps search all around for him and find him. But he is not far from any of us: 'By his power we live and move and exist.'

Acts 17:27–28a

Even after a tree dies, it can still stay standing for a long time. It looks alive, but it doesn't have any life in it. When people don't know Jesus, they are like trees with no life in them.

Jesus is the only one who can give us life. It's his power that brought us into existence and it's his life that fills us with our life. When we search for Jesus and put our trust in him, he gives us eternal life.

Because of God we live, move and having meaning! He is the reason we have eternal life and purpose on earth!

QUESTION TIME!

How do you know someone is alive?

Is it possible to be alive on the outside, but dead on the inside?

How do you know Jesus has given you eternal life?

What is the difference between being alive and having Jesus' life?

Dear God, I can have a beautiful life because you loved me and saved me. Thank you for giving me life and living in me.
Amen.

5

I AM YOUR GOOD SHEPHERD

I am the good shepherd. The good shepherd gives his life for the sheep.

John 10:11

In Bible times, being a shepherd was a hard job. A shepherd had to watch their sheep all day and night. Sometimes they even slept in the field with the sheep, just in case a bear or lion showed up. A good shepherd would defend the sheep with their own life!

Sheep are very hard to watch. They are constantly wandering around, helplessly getting lost, and needing help. At times we can be like sheep – in need of a good shepherd.

Jesus is our good shepherd because he watches over us every day and every night, even when we lose our way. When we needed to be saved from sin, Jesus gave his own life to set us free.

QUESTION TIME!

Do you think you'd like to be a shepherd if you lived in Bible times?

In what ways are you like a sheep? In what ways is Jesus like a shepherd?

What makes Jesus a good shepherd?

Why do you need a good shepherd to watch over you?

LET'S PRAY . . .

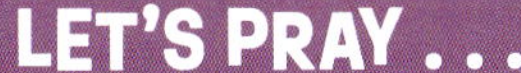

Dear God, thank you for being my good shepherd. I am grateful you loved me enough to give your own life to save me. Please continue to watch over me as I follow you!
Amen.

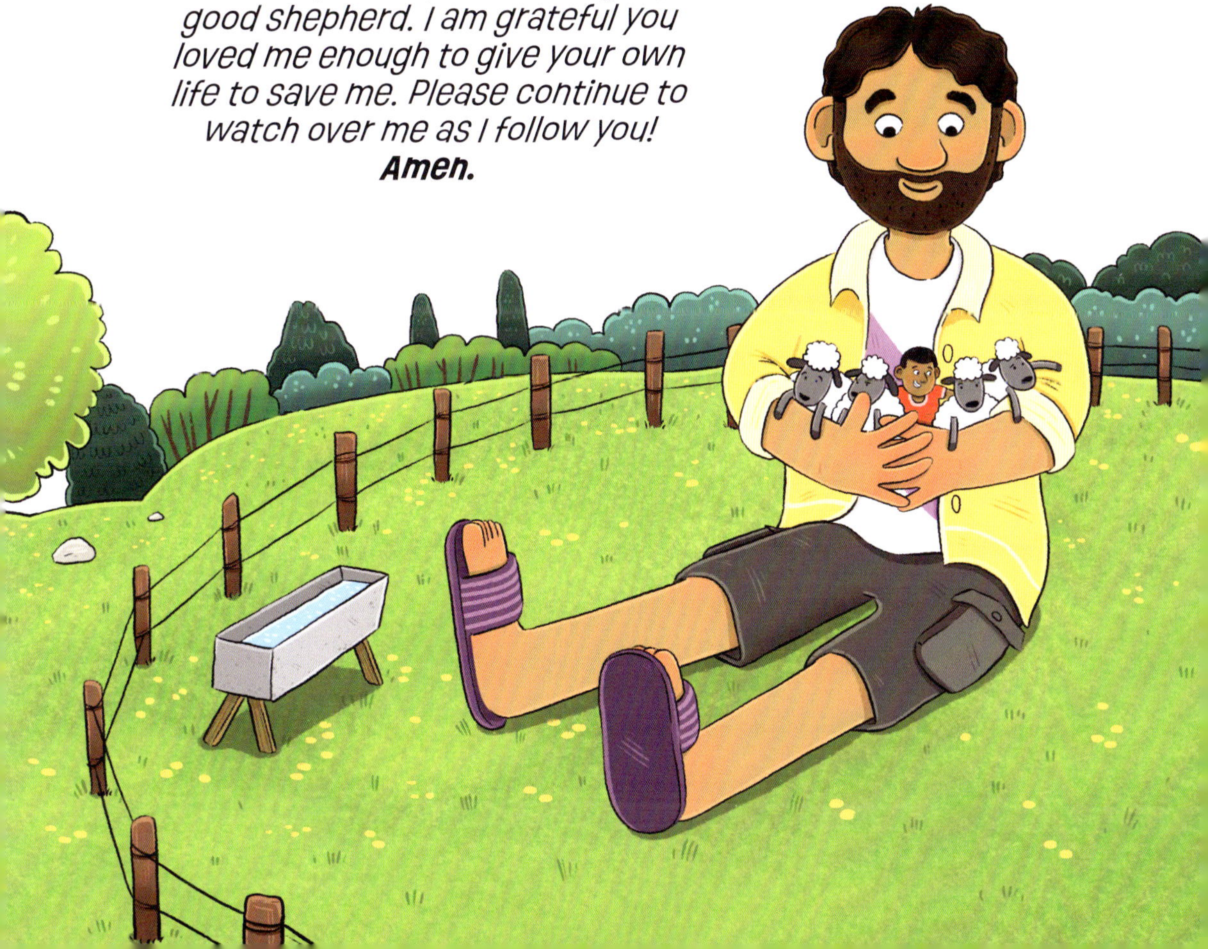

6

I AM YOUR PROVIDER

My God will use his wonderful riches in Christ Jesus to give you everything you need.

Philippians 4:19

To provide for someone means to give them what they need.

Sometimes what we want and what we need are different. When we don't get what we want, or what we ask for, we may think God hasn't provided for our needs.

When we feel this way, we can remember that God knows exactly what we need, and he promises to provide for us. Even if we don't always get what we want, we can trust that God will give us what we need!

QUESTION TIME!

What is the difference between what you need and what you want?

Why does God not always give us what we ask for?

What has God provided for you this week?

How can you remind yourself of God's promise to provide for your needs?

LET'S PRAY . . .

Dear God, thank you that you provide for me.
You are kind and I can trust you with all my needs even if I don't always get what I ask for.
Amen.

I AM YOUR SAVIOUR

I mean that while we were God's enemies, God made us his friends through the death of his Son. Surely, now that we are God's friends, God will save us through his Son's life.

Romans 5:10

When we choose not to follow Jesus, we are enemies with God. We are blind to our sin and our need for help! But God does not treat us like enemies. Even when we don't think we need a saviour, God's Son, Jesus, saves us from our sins!

Jesus turned us from enemies into FRIENDS when he died on the cross and rose to life again. He offers us freedom from sin, death, and despair.

Jesus saved us so that we can enjoy eternal peace, love, and life with God! Jesus is our great saviour.

QUESTION TIME!

Why do we need a saviour?

How did Jesus save us?

Why is it so great that Jesus is our saviour?

Would we be able to save ourselves without Jesus?

LET'S PRAY . . .

Dear God, thank you that you saved me. I'm happy that I get to be your friend and I'm thankful I get to spend forever with you. ***Amen.***

8

I AM YOUR STRENGTH

The Lord is my strength and shield. I trust him, and he helps me. I am very happy. And I praise him with my song.

Psalm 28:7

Although we might think we're strong, sometimes we will feel nervous, tired, or weak. But that's OK! Why? Because in those times, God will give us strength.

God is omnipotent, which means he is all-powerful. And the good news is that he shares his strength with us! When we trust God, he helps us!

In the moments we feel weak, God offers to be our strength. We can trust him to be strong even when we are not. Praise God for sharing his incredible strength with us!

QUESTION TIME!

Can you think of a time you needed strength when you felt weak?

Why do we need God's strength?

How does God share his strength with you?

Do you have a favourite song to sing to God? What is it?

LET'S PRAY . . .

Dear God, I praise you because you strengthen me when I feel weak. Thank you for helping me when I put my trust in you.
Amen.

I AM YOUR HELPER

I look up to the hills. But where does my help come from? My help comes from the Lord. He made heaven and earth.

Psalm 121:1–2

We all need help sometimes. We might need help being kind to others, or help with directions if we've got lost. We might even need help cheering up when we feel down.

It's not difficult to think of a time when each of us has needed help.

The Bible tells us to look to God because our help comes from him. He made heaven and earth, and he made us. He knows exactly what we need and when we need it. God can give us the help we need when we ask him.

QUESTION TIME!

Can you think of a time you needed help? Who helped you?

Do you find it easy to ask for help? Why or why not?

Have you ever asked God for help?

How does God help us?

LET'S PRAY . . .

Dear God, thank you that whenever I need help, you are there. Please help me to look to you and trust you to help when I struggle.

Amen.

I AM YOUR WARRIOR

But Moses answered, 'Don't be afraid! Stand still and see the Lord save you today. You will never see these Egyptians again after today. You will only need to remain calm. The Lord will fight for you.'

Exodus 14:13–14

Moses and the Israelites were trapped by Pharaoh and his great army. Just when they thought they would be destroyed, Moses encouraged the people by reminding them that God would fight for them.

When we feel afraid, we feel anxious, overwhelmed and nervous. These verses remind us that God is our warrior – he will fight for us when we cannot fight for ourselves.

Remember, God can save us, no matter what the situation might be. Sometimes the best thing we can do in the middle of a hard time is to be still, remain calm and trust that God is our warrior.

QUESTION TIME!

What do you do when you feel afraid and worried?

How does God fight for us?

Why can we trust God to be our warrior?

Have you ever asked God to help you in a difficult moment?

LET'S PRAY . . .

Dear God, thank you for being my warrior and fighting for me when I can't stand up for myself! Remind me that when I feel afraid, I can stay calm and ask you for help.

Amen.

11

I AM YOUR REST

Come to me, all of you who are tired and have heavy loads.
I will give you rest.

Matthew 11:28

Anyone who has ever carried something really heavy, like a big bag of groceries or a backpack filled with books, knows it's tiring! Carrying a heavy load causes our arms and legs to get tired and we need rest.

When we have a lot of worries on our minds, it's like we're carrying them in our hearts. Soon our hearts and minds get tired from carrying the worries and they need rest.

Jesus says that when we feel like we're carrying a heavy load, he will give us rest if we simply go to him through prayer.

QUESTION TIME!

Have you ever carried a very heavy load?

Why do you need rest from worries?

Why does Jesus offer you rest?

How does Jesus give you rest?

LET'S PRAY . . .

Jesus, thank you for giving me rest when I come to you. When my heart is tired, remind me to ask you for help and accept the rest you give.
Amen.

I AM YOUR REASON

God has made us what we are. In Christ Jesus, God made us new people so that we would do good works. God had planned in advance those good works for us. He had planned for us to live our lives doing them.

Ephesians 2:10

Have you ever wondered, *Why am I here?* or *What am I made for?*

The Bible says God made us who we are for a reason. He has made each one of us so that we would do good things. In fact, God has already planned good things for us to do in our lives!

God has given each one of us talents, gifts, interests and a purpose on earth. When we decide to participate in the good things God has planned for our lives, we will always have a reason to live each and every day.

QUESTION TIME!

What talents or interests do you have?

Why do you think God created you?

How do you know which good things God prepared for you to do?

How can trusting God's plan for your life give you purpose every day?

LET'S PRAY . . .

Dear God, thank you for creating me and preparing good things for me to do. You give me a reason to live each day!
Amen.

13

I AM YOUR TRUE LOVE

But Christ died for us while we were still sinners. In this way God shows his great love for us.

Romans 5:8

When you think of true love, you might think of fairy tales like Cinderella or *Shrek*. But do you know what true love is?

Jesus knows what true love is and he showed us when he sacrificed his life for ours on the cross to pay for our sins. Before we knew him or followed him, Jesus died for us. God's love doesn't depend on whether we love him or obey him.

God will always love us. Whether we're naughty or nice, dirty or clean, rich or poor, happy or sad! His love is unconditional. NOBODY loves us like God does!

QUESTION TIME!

Who do you love the most in the world?

What does unconditional love mean?

How does it make you feel knowing nobody loves you more than God loves you?

Have you ever felt like God's love for you depended on your behaviour?

LET'S PRAY . . .

Dear God, thank you for showing me what true love really is! Help me to love people unconditionally, just like you love them.
Amen.

I AM YOUR LIFE PRESERVER

I asked the Lord for help, and he answered me. He saved me from all that I feared.

Psalm 34:4

Have you ever felt so afraid it was hard to think of anything else? Sometimes being afraid feels like being tossed back and forth in a sea- a sea of fears. It can be hard to see any way to escape!

But, when it feels like we're drowning in a sea of fear, there is something we can do. We can ask God for help. He hears us and he will come to our rescue!

Just like a life preserver helps us stay safely above the water, God helps us feel safe from all our fears.

QUESTION TIME!

Do you ever feel afraid? What makes you feel afraid?

What do you do when you feel afraid?

What are some ways God helps calm your fears?

How can you practice trusting God to save you from fear?

LET'S PRAY . . .

Dear God, when I'm afraid please remind me that you hear me and want to save me from every fear.
Amen.

15

I AM YOUR COMFORTER

Praise be to the God and Father of our Lord Jesus Christ. God is the Father who is full of mercy. And he is the God of all comfort. He comforts us every time we have trouble, so that we can comfort others when they have trouble. We can comfort them with the same comfort that God gives us.

2 Corinthians 1:3–4

The Bible tells us that God is our comfort. He makes us feel better when we have trouble. He doesn't just comfort us occasionally; he comforts us EVERY time we have trouble, because he is the God of ALL comfort!

God's comfort isn't just for us, it's for others too. When God comforts us, he gives us the power to comfort others when they need it.

We can be sure that if we need comfort, God WILL be there for us.

QUESTION TIME!

Can you think of a time you were comforted by a friend or family member?

What does it feel like to be comforted?

How does God comfort you?

Who can you share God's comfort with today?

LET'S PRAY . . .

Dear God, thank you that you comfort me and make me feel better. Please show me how I can share your comfort with other people. ***Amen.***

16

I AM YOUR JUDGE

But the Lord rules forever.
He sits on his throne to judge.
The Lord will judge the world by what is right.
He will decide what is fair for the nations.

Psalm 9:7–8

A judge decides what is right or wrong in a courtroom. They get to decide who goes to prison and who goes free!

God is our judge because he decides what is right and wrong. God created the world and he will rule forever. So, what God says is right is way more important than what other people say is right.

When the world comes to an end, God is the only one who will have the power to judge our decisions and beliefs to decide who was right and wrong. When we want to know if something is right or wrong, we can ask God and he will tell us!

QUESTION TIME!

How do you decide if something is right or wrong?

Why is God the only one who has the power to judge?

How does God tell you what is right and wrong?

What things does God say are right? What things does God say are wrong?

LET'S PRAY . . .

Dear God, I am more interested in what you say is right than what other people think is right. Help me to listen to you and do what YOU say is right.

Amen.

I AM YOUR ROCK

So, trust the Lord always. Trust the Lord because he is our Rock forever.

Isaiah 26:4

Think of a BIG rock. Imagine it is so heavy, no one can move it, not even the Hulk! Even through wind and storms, that rock stays right where it is – it never moves.

God is like that great big rock! He will always be there for us and he can't be moved. No matter what we go through, God is our immovable rock forever and we can always trust him.

The worst storms, biggest mistakes, and strongest enemies don't stand a chance against God. Nothing and no one can move him away from us!

QUESTION TIME!

What is the biggest rock you've ever seen?

In what ways is God like a great big rock?

Why do we need God to be our rock?

Why can't anyone or anything move God away from us?

LET'S PRAY . . .

Dear God, thank you that you are my Rock through hard times and good times. I know nothing and no one will ever be able to move you. You will never leave me.

Amen.

I AM YOUR FRIEND

I don't call you servants now. A servant does not know what his master is doing. But now I call you friends because I have made known to you everything I heard from my Father.

John 15:15

When we think of a friend, do we think of someone who orders us around, or do we think of someone who shares their life with us and loves us?

We obey God and we serve him, but we are not JUST his servants. Jesus says that he is our friend, and we are HIS friends too! Jesus shares his thoughts, plans and life with us through the Bible. He loves us and he is the best friend we could ever have.

Through his friendship, we can share every day with someone who cares about us!

QUESTION TIME!

Can you think of someone you're friends with?

What makes someone a good friend?

What makes Jesus a good friend?

How can you deepen your friendship with Jesus?

LET'S PRAY . . .

Dear Jesus, thank you that you are my friend. I want to know you more and share every part of my life with you.
Amen.

19

I AM YOUR GIFT GIVER

Every good action and every perfect gift is from God. These good gifts come down from the Creator of the sun, moon, and stars. God does not change like their shifting shadows.

James 1:17

When we think of gifts, we might think of the presents wrapped under a Christmas tree or given at birthday parties.

God says EVERY good thing we enjoy is a gift from him! That means sunshine, good friends, and happy memories are all gifts! God loves giving us good things to enjoy.

If every good thing is a gift from God, that means God gives us gifts EVERY day. If we tried to count all the good things God has put around us, it would be impossible!

QUESTION TIME!

What is the best gift you've ever been given?

Can you name a few good things God has given you?

Why does God give us gifts?

What gift can you thank God for today?

LET'S PRAY . . .

Dear God, thank you for all the gifts you give me every day. I praise you because EVERY good thing comes from you!
Amen.

I AM YOUR LIGHT

Later, Jesus talked to the people again. He said, 'I am the light of the world. The person who follows me will never live in darkness. He will have the light that gives life.'

John 8:12

Have you ever tried doing something in the dark? Imagine trying to walk in a room that is completely dark. How easy is it to know where you're going when you can't see properly?

When we don't know where to go, what to do, or how to do something, we start to feel like we're in the dark. We need someone to turn a light on so we can find our way!

God says that he is our light, and when we follow him we will not live in darkness. By his light we can see where to go and how to live our lives!

QUESTION TIME!

Are you afraid of the dark?

Have you ever tried to do something in the dark? How did it go?

How does God give us light and what does it help us do?

When you feel like you're in the dark (feeling confused, scared, or alone), where can you find God's light?

LET'S PRAY . . .

Dear God, thank you that you light up my life! Without you, I am in the dark and I can't see. Please help me follow you always. ***Amen.***

I AM YOUR CREATOR

You made my whole being.
You formed me in my mother's body.
I praise you because you made me in an amazing and wonderful way. What you have done is wonderful.
I know this very well.

Psalm 139:13–14

Our mothers named us and raised us, but God knew us before we were even born!

God created each of us in an amazing and wonderful way. While we were still in our mother's womb, God formed us with a plan and purpose for our life. He made us all unique – beautiful in our own ways. When God looks at us, he sees his valuable creations.

God knew exactly what he was doing when he put us together. He took time, carefully blending our personalities, talents, gifts and appearance. His work is wonderful!

QUESTION TIME!

Do you think you were made wonderful and amazing?

Can you name something amazing that God created in you?

How do you think God feels about his creation?

How can you practise seeing yourself the way God sees you?

LET'S PRAY . . .

Dear God, thank you for caring for me, before I was even born. You have made me in an amazing and wonderful way! Help me to see myself the way you see me.

Amen.

22

I AM YOUR ETERNAL REFILL

And this hope will never disappoint us, because God has poured out his love to fill our hearts. God gave us his love through the Holy Spirit, whom God has given to us.

Romans 5:5

Some restaurants give free drink refills. As soon as a person finishes their drink, they can go back and refill their cup, again and again!

The Bible says God fills our hearts with love through the Holy Spirit. When we feel empty and in need of love, he fills us up again and again forever.

Imagine the amount of love God must have for us! If we let him fill us up with love every day, we will never run out of love for him, ourselves and the people around us.

QUESTION TIME!

If you could have free refills of one drink for the rest of your life, what would it be?

How do you get filled by God?

What happens when your heart is filled with love by God?

Why is it important that God fills your heart with love every day?

LET'S PRAY . . .

Dear God, thank you for filling me up with your love! I will never be empty of love because I know you will fill me up forever!

Amen.

23

I AM YOUR REDEEMER

I have swept away your sins like a big cloud.
I have removed your sins like a cloud that disappears into the air. Come back to me because I saved you.

Isaiah 44:22

When something is redeemed, what was broken is fixed. What used to have value is repaired and once again has value. For example, if a toy breaks, we can redeem it, by fixing it.

God's relationship with us, people, was broken because of sin. But instead of throwing us away, God decided to fix the relationship. God sent Jesus to earth to forgive our sins and make them disappear, just like clouds do!

God is our redeemer and he's asking us to come to him. He has swept away our sins and he is waiting with open arms, full of love!

QUESTION TIME!

Can you think of a time you fixed something that was broken?

What is your reaction to God making your sins disappear, like clouds?

How did God make our sins disappear?

Does God's love and forgiveness make you more or less likely to run into his open arms?

LET'S PRAY . . .

Dear God, thank you for making my sins disappear and fixing our relationship. I love you!
Amen.

24

I AM YOUR FOUNDATION

The foundation has already been built. No one can build any other foundation. The foundation that has already been laid is Jesus Christ.

1 Corinthians 3:11

What is a foundation? A foundation is what a building is built on. It's there to make sure the building doesn't come crashing down in a storm or during an earthquake!

Jesus is our strong foundation, and we can build our lives on him. When life is hard, he stops us from crashing down. Jesus holds us up; He helps us stay strong, and we can trust him as our foundation.

Imagine facing ANYTHING in life with Jesus as your solid, immovable foundation! With him as our foundation we will not crumble.

QUESTION TIME!

What is a building's foundation used for?

What can happen to a building if it doesn't have a strong foundation?

What do you depend on as your foundation to keep you strong?

How can Jesus be your strong foundation during hard times?

LET'S PRAY . . .

Dear God, thank you that you are my foundation. Help me to build my life on you so that I am secure, steady and strong, no matter what happens in life. ***Amen.***

I AM YOUR HEALER

He heals the brokenhearted. He bandages their wounds.

Psalm 147:3

God is our healer. He takes care of us and helps us heal from all kinds of illnesses.

God designed our bodies to heal, like broken bones coming back together and bruises disappearing after a few days. But he can also heal wounds we can't see, like broken hearts and hurt feelings.

When you find that you have a wound, don't be afraid to ask God to heal you. Whether your wound is physical, mental, or spiritual, he is powerful enough to heal ANY wound you bring to him.

QUESTION TIME!

Can you remember a time you had a wound – like a cut or blister – that needed healing?

What does it feel like when a wound heals?

Why is God's healing important?

Can you think of something you want God to heal in your life?

LET'S PRAY . . .

Dear God, thank you that you care for me. You are able to heal all my wounds. Help me to remember to ask you for healing when I am unwell.
Amen.

I AM YOUR KING

So God raised Christ to the highest place.
God made the name of Christ greater than every other name.
God wants every knee to bow to Jesus –
everyone in heaven, on earth, and under the earth.

Philippians 2:9–10

Kings have a lot of power. They are noble in the way they protect and lead the people of their country. If a peasant – common person – met the king, they would be expected to bow down, as a sign of respect.

God wants everyone to bow to Jesus because he is our king, the King of kings! Just like earthly kings receive respect from the people they lead, Jesus deserves our respect and admiration too.

Jesus is powerful, kind, and deserving of all our praise. He provides for all our needs, leads us with love, and gives us the honour of being part of his kingdom.

QUESTION TIME!

What rules would you make if you were a king or a queen?

What does a king do for their country?

How is Jesus similar to earthly kings? How is he different?

How can you show respect for King Jesus?

LET'S PRAY . . .

Dear God, you are greater than any king or ruler on earth! I give you praise because you are a strong and humble king. I will follow and adore you.
Amen.

I AM YOUR CAREGIVER

Give all your worries to him, because he cares for you.

1 Peter 5:7

Have you ever felt worried or scared? At times, events in life cause us to worry, and God wants us to remember that he will be there to help us.

God tells us to give ALL our worries to him because he cares deeply about us. When we give our worries and fears to him, he replaces them with peace.

If you ever feel like nobody cares about your worries, remember that God always cares. When we give him our worries, we don't have to worry about them anymore!

QUESTION TIME!

What worries or fears do you have?

How do you give your worries to God?

What happens when you give your worries to God?

Why does God want you to give your worries to him?

LET'S PRAY . . .

Dear God, today I give all my worries, fears, and anxieties to you. I know you will help me because you care for me. ***Amen.***

I AM YOUR MIRACLE WORKER

You are the God who did miracles.
You showed people your power.

Psalm 77:14

The Bible is FULL of stories describing God's miracles. Jesus walked on water, he made blind people see, he healed the sick, and he even rose from the dead!

God did lots of miracles in the past, and he still does miracles in our lives today. At times we forget the miracles we experience daily. Like the sun rising and setting, and being able to breathe and eat.

Sometimes when we ask for a miracle, we don't see it straight away. But we shouldn't give up praying! All things are possible with God and he will answer our prayers in the way he knows is best.

QUESTION TIME!

What is a miracle?

What miracles do you experience every day?

Have you ever prayed for God to do a miracle?

What is your favourite miracle in the Bible?

LET'S PRAY . . .

Dear God, I am amazed at the miraculous things you do. Thank you for the miracles you do every day! I trust you will answer my prayers in the best way.
Amen.

I AM YOUR WAY MAKER

This is what the Lord says. He is the one who made a road through the sea. Even through rough waters he made a path for his people.

Isaiah 43:16

Have you heard the story of God parting the Red Sea? The Israelites, God's people, were trying to escape Egypt, they were trapped, and all seemed hopeless. Then, God separated the Red Sea so the Israelites could cross on dry land and be free! He made a way for their escape.

Making a way for something means making it possible. God has a plan and purpose for our lives, and he can make a way even in the most impossible situations.

God can make a way for dreams to come true, broken relationships to be fixed and miracles to happen. Whatever it may be, we can trust God because he makes ways to succeed even when we think there is no way.

QUESTION TIME!

Have you ever felt like something you wanted was impossible or out of reach?

Can you think of something you would like God to make a way for?

Why is God able to make ways in impossible situations?

How can you practise trusting God when a situation seems impossible?

LET'S PRAY . . .

Dear God, thank you for being my way maker! Even if I think something seems impossible, like the Israelites crossing the Red Sea, show me your way to succeed.

Amen.

I AM YOUR WARM EMBRACE

If my father and mother leave me,
the Lord will take me in.

Psalm 27:10

Even if your mother and father leave you, God will embrace you, he will take you in.

Mothers and fathers are the closest family members we have. But sometimes, they aren't around. Sometimes our parents are unable to be with us, or they choose to leave.

Even if the people who have known us the longest leave, God will not. And even if the people who were supposed to love us the most don't, God will. He will take us in his arms and be with us. God will care for us as a mother and father should, with his deep love.

QUESTION TIME!

Who cares for you at home?

Why is it important to be loved and cared for?

What does it mean to be 'embraced' by God?

How does God's warm embrace change our life?

LET'S PRAY . . .

Dear God, you embrace me and care for me even when the people closest to me leave. Thank you for being someone I can depend on.

Amen.

31

I AM YOUR STAIN REMOVER

The Lord says,
'Come, we will talk these things over.
Your sins are red like deep red cloth.
But they can be as white as snow.
Your sins are bright red.
But you can be white like wool.'

Isaiah 1:18

Have you ever had a stain on your clothes you couldn't wash out? What did you do with the clothes? If stains don't come out, the clothes are usually thrown away.

Did you know, just like clothes, we can get stained too? It happens every time we disobey God. The good thing is, God would never consider throwing us away, because he loves us. He easily removes the toughest, dirtiest stains.

When we disobey God and get stained, all we need to do is ask for forgiveness. God can forgive ANY mistake, no matter how big or small.

QUESTION TIME!

Have you ever stained your clothes?

Why does sinning/disobeying God leave a stain?

How does God wash away our stains – sins?

Is there a 'stain' or sin you'd like to ask God to forgive today?

LET'S PRAY . . .

Dear God, thank you for forgiving me and washing all the stains away! I praise you for your power over my mistakes.

Amen.

I AM YOUR CONFIDENCE

Jesus looked at them and said, 'For men this is impossible. But for God all things are possible.'

Matthew 19:26

Confidence is when you feel like you can trust yourself. For example, you can have confidence in your ability to sing happy birthday because you have practised it 1,000 times!

There are times we face challenges that we don't have the ability to overcome on our own. When this happens, Jesus tells us we can have confidence in him.

So, when we don't have confidence, or trust in ourselves, we can have complete confidence in God! He is able to help us, because nothing is impossible for him.

QUESTION TIME!

Can you think of something you feel confident in doing?

Can you think of a time you didn't feel confident?

Why is it important we look to God for confidence?

How can we learn to trust God and have confidence in him?

LET'S PRAY . . .

Dear God, even when the challenges I face feel impossible, thank you that all things are possible for you! You are my confidence and I trust you. ***Amen.***

I AM YOUR LISTENING EAR

The Lord is close to everyone who prays to him, to all who truly pray to him.

Psalm 145:18

Do you like being judged or interrupted when you speak? Of course not! We want to feel seen, heard and loved when we speak to others.

Thankfully we always have someone who is ready to listen – it's God! God promises that if we pray, talk to him, he will listen carefully.

Whenever we need someone to talk to, and we're not sure who to go to, God is available. He will listen to whatever we want to say.

QUESTION TIME!

Who do you like talking to most?

Have you ever felt like you didn't have someone to talk to? How did it feel?

Why do you think God wants to talk to you?

Is there anything you want to talk to God about today?

LET'S PRAY . . .

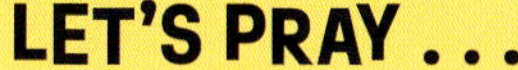

Dear God, thank you for being there for me when I need someone to talk to. You listen to me with love and answer my prayers!
Amen.

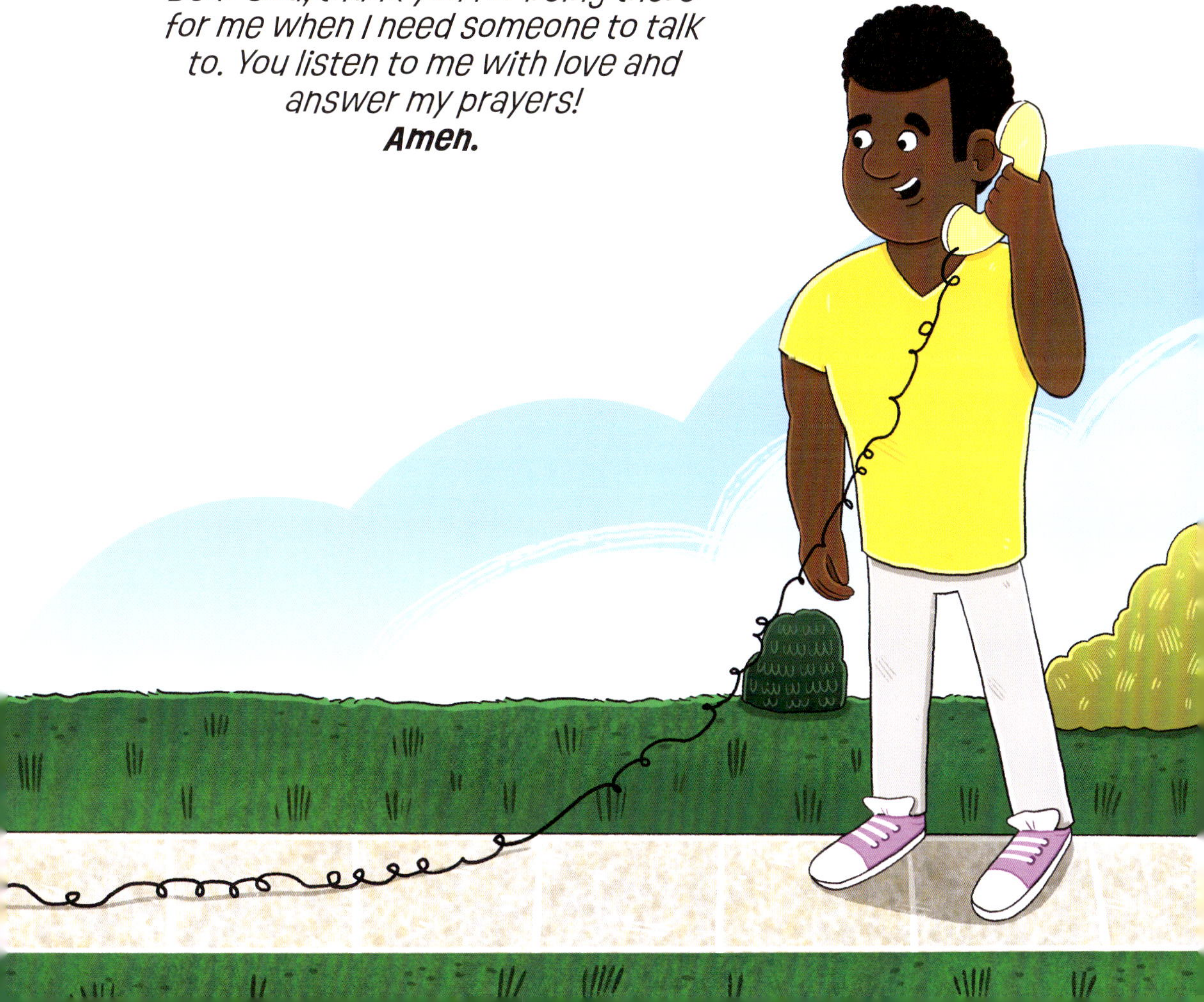

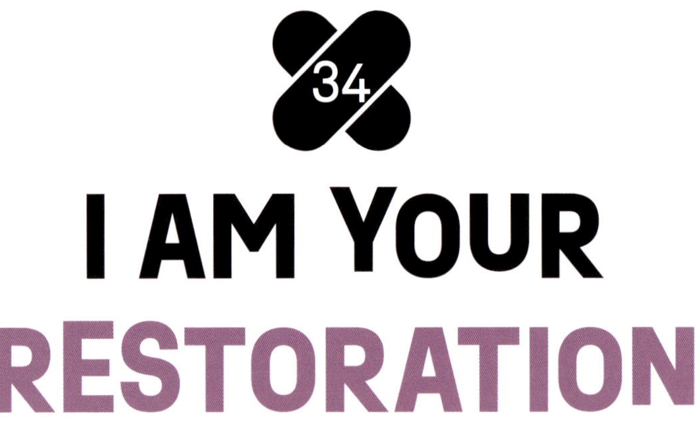

I AM YOUR RESTORATION

You have given me many troubles and bad times. But you will give me life again.

Psalm 71:20a

Restoration happens when something that is bad is made good again. For example, when a home is destroyed by an earthquake or fire, it is no longer usable or safe. But when it is rebuilt – restored – it is once again safe and warm!

God works in similar ways in our lives. When we experience painful events, we might feel broken and useless. But God can restore us, so that he can use us again.

God gives us joy after sadness, strength after weakness and courage after fear. He is our restoration.

QUESTION TIME!

Have you ever turned a bad situation into something good?

Can you think of an example of something that's been damaged being restored?

How does God restore you when you feel broken?

Why does God restore you?

LET'S PRAY . . .

Dear God, I praise you because you have the power to bring restoration. You are able to make all things new again – including me!
Amen.

I AM YOUR IDENTITY

But you are chosen people. You are the King's priests. You are a holy nation. You are a nation that belongs to God alone. God chose you to tell about the wonderful things he has done. He called you out of darkness into his wonderful light.

1 Peter 2:9

What is your identity? Your identity is who you really are.

An Identification Card (an ID) has basic information on it, like your name, birthday and height. These pieces of information help identify who you are.

Sometimes people want to tell us who we are. Some people say nice things and others say mean things. It can be hard to know what to believe when we let them define us.

But God chose us and knows us. What he says is more important than what anyone else says about us. God made us and gave us our true identity.

QUESTION TIME!

Can you name a few things that make you who you are?

What does God say about your identity?

Is it easier to believe what God says or what people say about you?

How can you remind yourself of your God-given identity every day?

LET'S PRAY . . .

Dear God, thank you for making me
who I am and giving me my identity.
Because of you I am valuable and loved.
Amen.

36

I AM YOUR ADVOCATE

My dear children, I write this letter to you so that you will not sin. But if anyone does sin, we have Jesus Christ to help us. He is the Righteous One. He defends us before God the Father.

1 John 2:1

What is an advocate? An advocate is somebody who stands up for another person and defends them. Kind of like a lawyer defends someone in a courtroom.

When we sin, we deserve punishment. But when Jesus died on the cross, he took the punishment for our sins once and for all.

Because Jesus was punished and forgave our sins, he made us righteous, claimed our innocence and set us free. Now, whenever we sin, Jesus defends us. Without him, we wouldn't be able to defend ourselves.

QUESTION TIME!

Have you ever been worried you would get in trouble for something you did?

Why do you need Jesus to defend you before God?

Why can't you defend yourself?

How does it make you feel that Jesus set you free from sin?

LET'S PRAY . . .

Dear God, I'm sorry for the times I sin and choose not to obey you. Thank you for defending and forgiving me. Because of you I am innocent and do not need to fear punishment.

Amen.

37

I AM YOUR SHIELD

So our hope is in the Lord. He is our help,
our shield to protect us.

Psalm 33:20

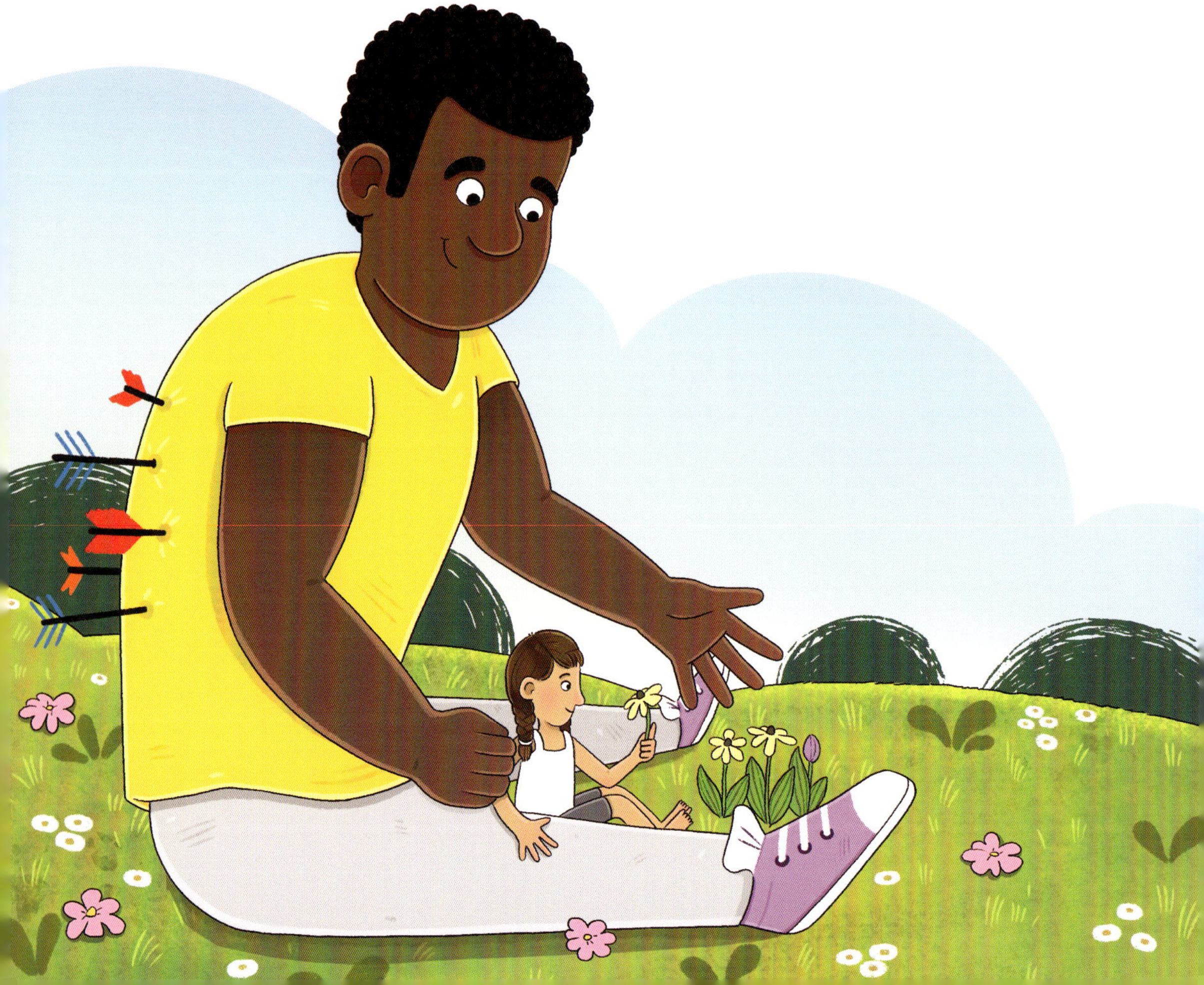

What does a shield do? It is used to protect the person using it from getting injured by something harmful or dangerous, like an arrow or a sword.

God wants to be our shield. He wants to, and is able to, protect us from things that would hurt us.

Sometimes we feel pain and wonder where God's protection is. There are times God chooses not to shield us from everything that could hurt us.

During the times we don't understand why we're experiencing hurt or why God isn't shielding us, we should talk to him. Then God can comfort us, answer our questions and fill us with hope again.

QUESTION TIME!

Have you ever used a shield?

How does God shield us from hurt?

Why do we sometimes get hurt even though God is our shield?

Is there anything you want God to shield you from right now?

LET'S PRAY . . .

Dear God, thank you for being my shield and for protecting me. You are awesome. Please remind me to talk to you when I feel confused or discouraged.
Amen.

38

I AM YOUR ANCHOR

We have this hope as an anchor for the soul, sure and strong.
It enters behind the curtain in the Most Holy Place in heaven.

Hebrews 6:19

An anchor is used to keep a boat in place, so the wind and waves don't sweep it away.

Sometimes we face difficult challenges in life that could sweep us away from God and cause us to forget his goodness. But Jesus is our anchor. When we trust him, he will strengthen us during the worst storms of life.

We are the boat and Jesus is our anchor. As long as we trust in him, nothing in life will be able to take us away from his love and his good plan for our lives.

QUESTION TIME!

Why is it important to have an anchor in a storm?

What can sweep you away from God in life?

When you experience a difficult moment, how can Jesus be your anchor?

Why can we trust Jesus to be our anchor?

LET'S PRAY . . .

Dear God, thank you for being my anchor when hard times come! You give me hope for the future. Help me to hold on to you as my anchor.
Amen.

I AM YOUR FORGIVENESS

But if we confess our sins, he will forgive our sins. We can trust God. He does what is right. He will make us clean from all the wrongs we have done.

1 John 1:9

Everything we do has consequences. If we squeeze a balloon too hard, the consequence will be that it bursts! The Bible says the consequence of sin is separation from God.

When we disobey God's commandments, we deserve punishment for what we've done. The good news is that Jesus was punished for our sins. He took our place and now he can forgive all our sins so we don't have to be separated from God.

Jesus forgives EVERY wrong thing we've ever done when we ask him to. He never gets tired of forgiving us when we say, 'I'm sorry.'

QUESTION TIME!

Can you think of a time you disobeyed a rule?

What does separation from God mean?

Why do you need forgiveness from God?

Is there anything you'd like to ask God to forgive today?

LET'S PRAY . . .

Dear God, thank you for forgiving me
EVERY TIME I confess my sins to you.
Help me say sorry when I know I've done
the wrong thing and disobeyed you.
Amen.

I AM YOUR BROTHER

God knew them before he made the world.
And God chose them to be like his Son.
Then Jesus would be the firstborn of many brothers.

Romans 8:29

Have you ever thought about Jesus as your brother? Well, if Jesus is the Son of God and we are the children of God, then Jesus is our brother! We are all part of his family.

God, our heavenly Father, treats us with the same love and acceptance as he treats Jesus. As God's children, we get to experience being part of a family that supports, loves and protects us.

We have an older brother, Jesus, who is looking out for us, helping us through life and cheering us on. He teaches us about life and shows us by example. Jesus is our brother, who we can put all our hope and trust in.

QUESTION TIME!

Do you have older brothers or sisters?

How does an older brother/sister help their younger siblings?

Why is Jesus the best older brother?

What do you enjoy about being part of God's family?

LET'S PRAY . . .

Dear God, thank you that you have made me part of your family. I am thankful you have given me every good thing, the same as you give Jesus!
Amen.

41 I AM YOUR SOLID GROUND

I waited patiently for the Lord. He turned to me and heard my cry. He lifted me out of the pit of destruction, out of the sticky mud. He stood me on a rock. He made my feet steady.

Psalm 40:1–2

Walking on mud can be hard because it's sticky, slippery and easy to get stuck in. Trying to walk when your feet are stuck takes a lot of time and effort. It's tiring!

Sometimes sad events happen in life and we feel stuck in the sadness, like getting stuck in mud. We try to move forward, but it's hard. When we feel stuck, God is the one who picks us up and puts us on solid ground.

When God puts us on solid ground, we are free to move forward and find joy, without being held back. If we ever feel stuck, we can pray to God and he will be our solid ground.

QUESTION TIME!

Have you ever been stuck in the mud? How did it feel?

What is the difference between walking on mud and walking on solid ground?

What kinds of events can make us feel stuck in sadness?

Why is God our solid ground?

LET'S PRAY . . .

Dear God, thank you for hearing me, lifting me out of the mud, and standing me on solid ground! Because of you I am free!
Amen.

42

I AM YOUR VICTORY

You can get the horses ready for battle.
But it is the Lord who gives the victory.

Proverbs 21:31

In a competition, who receives the victory? Is it the best person, the smartest person, or maybe the strongest person?

Although we should work hard in everything we do, God reminds us that he is ultimately the one who gives us the victory. Sometimes what happens (as we trust God) depends more on God's plan than how hard we try to succeed or win.

Victory doesn't just refer to someone who's won a competition. God can give us the victory in our personal goals, internal struggles and daily tasks. So, if you're facing a challenge you'd like to overcome, ask God to give you victory!

QUESTION TIME!

Have you ever wanted to win or succeed at something? What was it?

Have you ever won at a game? How or why did you win?

How does God give us victory over goals, struggles and daily tasks?

Why does God have the power to give us victory?

LET'S PRAY . . .

Dear God, I praise you because you are the one who can give me victory. Help me to trust in you when I face challenges and need the victory.
Amen.

43

I AM YOUR GARDENER

I am the true vine; my Father is the gardener. He cuts off every branch of mine that does not produce fruit. And he trims and cleans every branch that produces fruit so that it will produce even more fruit.

John 15:1–2

Each part of our life is like a branch. Our friendships, hobbies and after-school activities are all branches. Some branches connect us to God and some branches turn us away from him.

God wants us to be close to him so that our lives are full of good 'fruit' like love, joy and peace. Sometimes God cuts off a branch in our lives because it's pulling us away from him. He does this because he loves us and wants the best for us!

Seeing parts of our lives change or disappear can be very difficult. We can find encouragement knowing that God allows change to draw us close to him and produce more good fruit.

QUESTION TIME!

Can you think of a time when something in your life ended or changed?

What are some 'branches' in your life?

Why does God remove things from our lives?

What kind of good fruit does God want to produce in us?

LET'S PRAY . . .

Dear God, you are the gardener and I am a branch. I trust that you know how to bring me close to you and produce good things from my life, even when it's difficult.
Amen.

I AM YOUR MASTER

And you should not be called 'Master.' You have only one Master, the Christ.

Matthew 23:10

In Bible times, a master was a person who had servants. The servants had to do anything the master told them to do. We may not have a master ordering us around, but we do have teachers, presidents, prime ministers and police officers who tell us what to do.

It's good to respect and obey people in authority, but we should also remember Jesus is the master of the universe. We should listen to Jesus and obey him above anyone else.

If the government, our teachers, or even our parents tell us to do something different than what Jesus says in the Bible, we should listen to Jesus instead. He is our only master!

QUESTION TIME!

What 'masters' do you have telling you what to do?

What should you do if people in charge make rules that go against God's rules?

Why should you listen to Jesus above anyone else?

How can we serve God, our master, well?

LET'S PRAY . . .

Dear God, there is no one who has more power than you do. I will choose to listen to you and obey you above anyone else.
Amen.

I AM YOUR SHELTER

Those who go to God Most High for safety will be protected by God All-Powerful. I will say to the Lord, 'You are my place of safety and protection. You are my God, and I trust you.

Psalm 91:1–2

A shelter protects us from our surroundings. It gives us a place to stay dry when it rains, keep warm when it's cold and stay safe when there's danger.

The writer of Psalm 91 experienced God as his shelter, a safe place where he could find protection. When he felt afraid, he could call out, 'God, you are my safety and my protection.'

God is a safe place, a shelter, where we find protection. We can trust him to look after us. So, when we feel afraid, we remember that God is our shelter!

QUESTION TIME!

Where do you choose to go when you're looking for safety?

Why is it important to have a safe shelter?

What makes God a good shelter?

When you feel afraid, how can you remind yourself that God is your shelter?

LET'S PRAY . . .

Dear God, you are my safe shelter.
Help me to trust you for my safety
and protection.
Amen.

I AM YOUR INSTRUCTOR

All Scripture is inspired by God and is useful for teaching and for showing people what is wrong in their lives. It is useful for correcting faults and teaching how to live right.

2 Timothy 3:16

Instructions are important if we want to learn how to do something new. They show us what to do and how to do it. Someone who gives instructions is called an instructor. For example, teachers are called 'instructors'.

When we decide to follow Jesus, there are a lot of lessons we should learn about how to follow him. And the only instructor capable to teach us how to do that is God himself!

God gave us the Bible, Scripture, to instruct us how to follow Jesus and live a life that pleases him. In the Bible we find answers to our questions, advice on how to live and guidelines to follow so we can live meaningful lives.

QUESTION TIME!

Can you talk about a time you followed instructions? How did the instructions help you?

Why did God give you the Bible?

Why do you need instructions to follow Jesus?

What does it mean to live a meaningful life?

LET'S PRAY . . .

Dear God, thank you for giving me instructions so I can be like Jesus and live a meaningful life. Remind me to read the Bible and learn from it! ***Amen.***

47

I AM YOUR PROTECTOR

The Lord is good.
He gives protection in times of trouble.
He knows who trusts in him.

Nahum 1:7

God is the strongest, most powerful being in the universe. If he is protecting us, what is there to be scared of? Nothing and no one can overthrow God.

Knowing this about God should make us very happy. We have the strongest guy on OUR team and nobody can defeat him!

Anytime we feel afraid and we need protection, we can trust God. He is good and he is strong enough to protect us from whatever we fear.

QUESTION TIME!

What does a protector do?

Have you ever protected someone or something?

Can you think of a time when God protected you from trouble?

Do you feel more brave knowing that God is your protector?

LET'S PRAY . . .

Dear God, thank you for your strength and protection. I'm happy that nothing and no one is too big or strong for you.
Amen.

48

I AM YOUR RIGHTEOUSNESS

God makes people right with himself through their faith in Jesus Christ. This is true for all who believe in Christ, because all are the same.

Romans 3:22

Righteousness means being right or being good. In the Bible, the word 'righteous' is used to describe a person who obeys God's commands.

It's impossible to obey God's commands ALL the time, because we struggle with sin. So how can we be righteous? God says, we can be righteous through faith in Jesus because he defeated our sin and offers us his own righteousness!

God is pleased when we obey him, but being righteous isn't just about having good behaviour or avoiding bad behaviour. True righteousness only comes through faith in Jesus and his victory over sin.

QUESTION TIME!

Why do you do good things?

Can you think of examples of righteous behaviour?

Is it possible to be righteous without Jesus' help?

Why does your faith in Jesus make you righteous?

LET'S PRAY . . .

Dear God, thank you for defeating sin and covering me with your righteousness. My faith is in you, not in my own good actions!
Amen.

I AM YOUR BUILDER

If the Lord doesn't build the house, the builders are working for nothing. If the Lord doesn't guard the city, the guards are watching for nothing.

Psalm 127:1

Have you ever built a sandcastle on the beach? When the waves come, the castle is washed away! All the work put into making the castle is gone.

Putting a lot of work into something without including God is like building a sandcastle that gets washed away in a few hours. When we put our time and effort into projects without God, we miss out on the opportunity to build something eternal with him!

We can always invite God to build with us. None of our time or effort will be wasted if God is building beside us.

QUESTION TIME!

Have you ever tried building a castle in the sand?

In what ways can we actively include God in our plans?

Why should we always include God in our plans and projects?

What can we build with God that lasts forever?

LET'S PRAY . . .

Dear God, I want to include you in everything I do. And I want to be part of what you're building! Thank you for being in my life.

Amen.

I AM YOUR DOOR

I am the door. The person who enters through me will be saved. He will be able to come in and go out and find pasture.

John 10:9

Doors can lead us anywhere. You probably have a door to your bedroom, to the bathroom, to your car and to your classroom at school.

But why is Jesus calling himself a door? He's our door because anyone who goes through him will be saved. That means, anyone who puts their faith and trust in Jesus will be saved from living life without God!

Accepting Jesus' invitation to come through him opens a door to experiencing life with God. Jesus offers us joy, love, peace and every good thing! Jesus is the best door we could ever go through.

QUESTION TIME!

Can you name a few places that doors can lead to?

Have you ever been surprised by what was on the other side of a door?

How do we go through Jesus, our door?

What do we experience when we go through Jesus, our door?

LET'S PRAY . . .

Dear God, thank you for being my door to salvation! When I trust you, I find every good thing.
Amen.

I AM YOUR ENCOURAGER

So don't worry, because I am with you. Don't be afraid, because I am your God. I will make you strong and will help you. I will support you with my right hand that saves you.

Isaiah 41:10

Kind words, or encouragement, can give us energy. It can make us brave when we feel nervous or shy. Encouragement can also help us do difficult things, especially when we feel like giving up.

God is our encourager. He encourages us by telling us he is present and helping us. We don't need to worry or be afraid, because God will make us strong and support us!

The Bible is full of encouragement from God to help us. He is always ready to give us encouragement when we need support.

QUESTION TIME!

Can you think of a time you felt a bit nervous and needed encouragement?

Have you ever encouraged someone?

How does God encourage us?

Can you think of a Bible verse that encourages you?

LET'S PRAY . . .

Dear God, please encourage me when I feel nervous or scared. I won't be afraid because you will help and support me. Your encouragement gives me strength! ***Amen.***

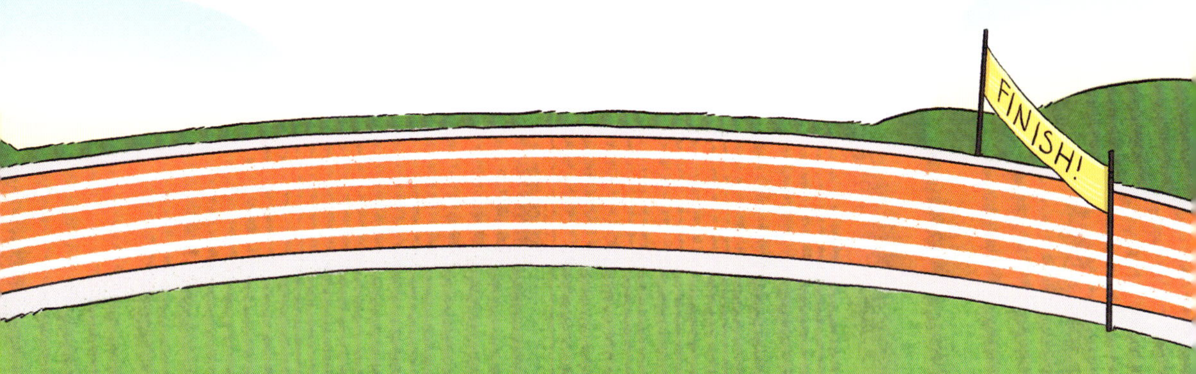

52 i

I AM YOUR EXAMPLE

Do not be angry with each other, but forgive each other. If someone does wrong to you, then forgive him. Forgive each other because the Lord forgave you.

Colossians 3:13

If a person wants to become a professional football player, they will probably look at other professional football players as examples and imitate what they do.

If we want to live a life that honours God, we should follow Jesus' example. Jesus loved and forgave everyone, even the people who did bad things to him. Jesus even forgave the Roman soldiers who killed him!

If we let go of our angry feelings and forgive the people who hurt us, we are following Jesus' example. The Bible reminds us that God forgives all the bad things we do, so we should also forgive the bad things others do – even when it's hard!

QUESTION TIME!

Have you ever followed someone's example? (A friend, celebrity, family member?)

Have you ever had to forgive someone? Was it hard or easy to forgive them?

Why is it sometimes difficult to forgive people who do bad things to us?

How does forgiving those who hurt us honour God?

LET'S PRAY . . .

Dear God, thank you that Jesus is a perfect example of how to live life. Help me to forgive others just like Jesus forgives me.
Amen.

I AM YOUR PROMISE KEEPER

It's almost time for me to die. You know and fully believe that the Lord has done great things for you. You know that he has not failed in any of his promises. He has kept every promise he has given.

Joshua 23:14

A man called Joshua is speaking in this verse. He's getting old and is ready to go to heaven, but before he goes, he wants to tell everyone about how God keeps his promises.

Joshua experienced God keep lots of promises. When Joshua's small army had to fight against a big army of giants, God promised that they would still win. And they did! So, Joshua knew that whatever God promised was going to come true.

We can trust in every promise God makes because he will never break them. No matter how long it takes, God will keep his promises.

QUESTION TIME!

Have you ever made a promise to someone?

What promises does God make to us in the Bible?

What is your favourite promise from God?

Why is it important that God keeps his promises?

LET'S PRAY . . .

Dear God, I am so thankful you keep all your promises. When I start to doubt you, help me to remember you are a promise keeper!
Amen.

I AM YOUR NEW BEGINNING

If anyone belongs to Christ, then he is made new. The old things have gone; everything is made new!

2 Corinthians 5:17

Did you know butterflies start their lives crawling along the ground as caterpillars? Once they transform into butterflies, it's hard to believe they were ever caterpillars at all, because they are different in almost every way!

When we decide to follow Jesus, he transforms us. Jesus gives us a new heart, identity, focus, and a new beginning! When Jesus makes us new, we can see life in a whole new way.

Butterflies don't crawl on the ground after they've come out of their cocoon. Once Jesus gives us a new beginning, we don't go back to the way we were before we met Jesus.

QUESTION TIME!

Have you ever received something new? What was it?

How does God make us new?

What evidence can you see when God makes you new?

Why do we need God to make us new?

LET'S PRAY . . .

Dear God, thank you that you make me new! You have changed me completely and given me a new identity.
Amen.

I AM YOUR HIDING PLACE

You are my hiding place.
You protect me from my troubles.
You fill me with songs of salvation.

Psalm 32:7

There are a lot of reasons we might want to hide – fear, embarrassment, or uncertainty. There are many places we could hide, like behind the sofa or behind our friends.

God is the best hiding place when we want to hide or just need time to think. He protects us from trouble and reminds us that we are his children, and we are saved.

So, when we need somewhere to hide, we can go to God. As well as giving us space to hide, he gives us encouragement and fills us with joy!

QUESTION TIME!

Have you ever wanted a place to hide?

What kinds of things make people want to hide? Can you think of an example?

Why is God a good hiding place for you?

How can you hide in God?

LET'S PRAY . . .

Dear God, you are the best hiding place for me because you protect me and remind me that I am safe and loved. Thank you.
Amen.

56

I AM YOUR GUIDE

But when the Spirit of truth comes he will lead you into all truth. He will not speak his own words. He will speak only what he hears and will tell you what is to come.

John 16:13

It's common to hear people say, 'Follow your heart', but this idea doesn't come from the Bible. Instead of letting our hearts guide us, Jesus wants to guide us. He wants us to listen to and follow the Holy Spirit.

Although we may be tempted to follow our own desires and ideas, God knows us better than we know ourselves. He is the best guide for our lives because he created the world and he made us.

We can trust God's guidance because he knows what's best for us and he only speaks the truth.

QUESTION TIME!

Have you ever got lost? Who or what were you following?

Is it easy or hard to follow God? Why?

How can you tell if an idea is from God or from yourself?

Why is God the best guide you could ever have?

LET'S PRAY . . .

Dear God, thank you for sending me the Holy Spirit as my guide. I know I can follow you because you made everything, and you only speak truth!
Amen.

57

I AM YOUR HIGH PRIEST

We have a great high priest who has gone into heaven. He is Jesus the Son of God. So let us hold on to the faith we have. For our high priest is able to understand our weaknesses. He was tempted in every way that we are, but he did not sin.

Hebrews 4:14–15

We have a lot of different experiences in life. At times we have experiences we think nobody else would ever understand, not even our closest friends.

Although Jesus is our high priest, the Son of God, and holy in every way, he is familiar with pain and weakness. Jesus understands everything we go through. He experienced life on earth and was tempted in every way.

So, even if we feel we've been through something nobody else would understand, Jesus understands. We can find encouragement talking to him.

QUESTION TIME!

What does it mean to be tempted?

Have you experienced anything you think Jesus wouldn't understand?

Why is it important Jesus lived life on earth and was 'tempted in every way'?

How does Jesus help you when you feel tempted or experience weakness?

LET'S PRAY . . .

Dear God, when I feel like nobody sees or understands me, thank you that you always do. No matter what I go through, you understand.
Amen.

I AM YOUR FAITHFUL ONE

God is faithful. He is the One who has called you to share life with his Son, Jesus Christ our Lord.

1 Corinthians 1:9

What does it mean to be faithful? When someone is faithful, it means they keep the promises they make.

If you go to the cinema with God and he promises to save you a seat, he will. It doesn't matter how long you wait for popcorn, how busy the cinema gets, or even if you miss half the movie. When you get back, God will still be there with the seat he saved for you!

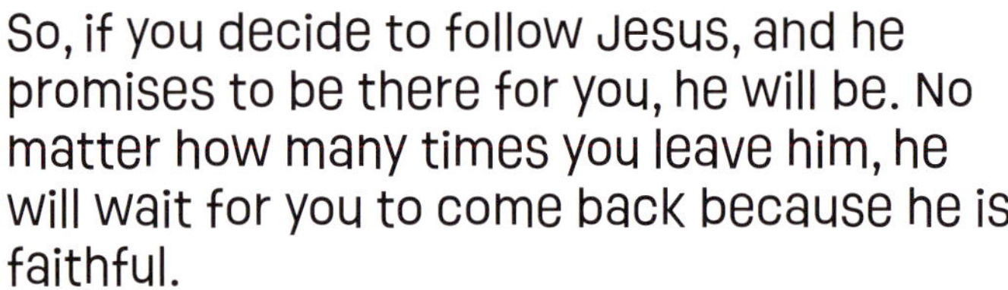

So, if you decide to follow Jesus, and he promises to be there for you, he will be. No matter how many times you leave him, he will wait for you to come back because he is faithful.

QUESTION TIME!

Have you ever been faithful to a friend or kept a promise to them?

Why is it good that Jesus is faithful to us?

What would it look like for you to be faithful to Jesus?

What promises does God keep to you?

LET'S PRAY . . .

Dear God, thank you for being faithful to me no matter what happens in life. Help me to be faithful to you too!
Amen.

I AM YOUR FREEDOM

So if the Son makes you free, then you will be truly free.

John 8:36

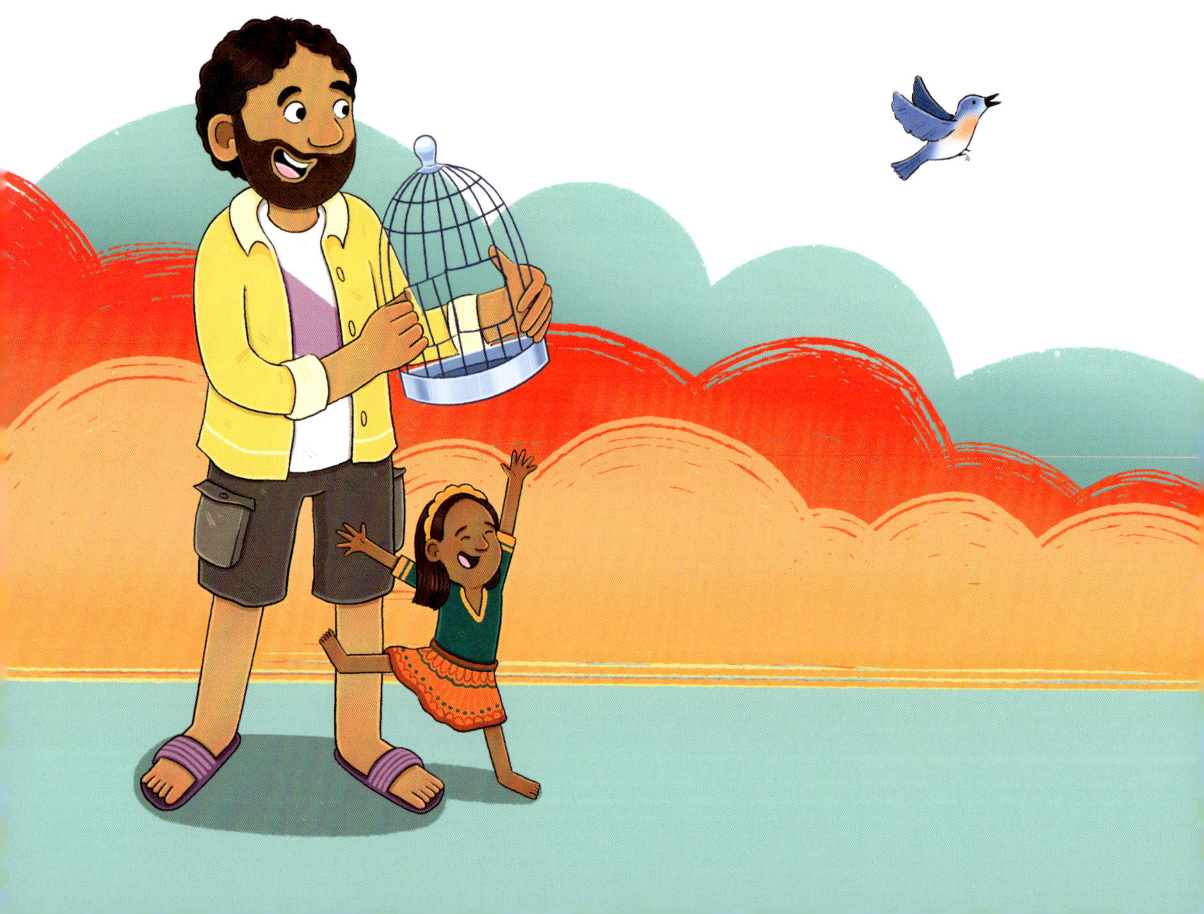

Is a bird in a cage free? It's free to move around the cage, but it's not free to fly.

When God sets us free, we can soar on wings like eagles! We are filled with hope. The situations in life which surround us don't determine our worth, mood, or future hope.

God sets us free from sin so that we can enjoy the life he created for each of us. So, if God sets us free, we are truly free! And nothing can stop us from freely loving and enjoying our relationship with God.

QUESTION TIME!

What do you think it means to be free?

What does God set us free from?

How does God set us free?

Why do we need God to set us free?

LET'S PRAY . . .

Dear God, thank you for setting me free from things that are not good for me. Remind me each morning that I am free in Jesus!
Amen.

60

I AM YOUR STRONG TOWER

The Lord is like a strong tower. Those who do what is right can run to him for safety.

Proverbs 18:10

In Bible times, cities had towers to keep watch. There would always be a guard in the tower looking out for enemy armies. If an enemy was coming, the guard would warn the people in the city. Then, they would run and find protection inside the tower.

God is like a strong tower, because he is always watching over us. We may not need to run away from an enemy army, but we still experience trouble and need a place we can run to for safety.

Finding safety in God means being confident that he loves us, has the power to protect us and has good plans for our lives.

QUESTION TIME!

Have you ever been to the top of a very tall building, and looked over a whole city or landscape?

What kind of troubles makes us run to God?

How can you know God loves you and offers you safety?

How does it make you feel that God is always watching over you?

LET'S PRAY . . .

Dear God, help me remember that you are watching over me. Thank you that when I am in trouble, I can run to you. ***Amen.***

61

I AM YOUR CONSTANT

Jesus Christ is the same yesterday, today, and forever.

Hebrews 13:8

As we look around, everything seems to change. The seasons change, our friends change, and even we change as we get older!

But there is someone who never changes, and never will. God is the same yesterday, today and FOREVER. He never changes, he is constant.

When we experience change it can be difficult and confusing, because we don't know what to expect. But with God, we know what to expect because he is our constant. Even if everything around us changes, he never will. His love never changes, his kindness never fades and his promises are true forever.

QUESTION TIME!

Do you like change? Why or why not?

Can you remember a time you experienced a big change?

Why does God never change?

Can you name something about God that never changes?

LET'S PRAY . . .

Dear God, thank you that no matter what I go through, you never change. I can always count on you to be there for me. ***Amen.***

62

I AM YOUR COUNSELLOR

This lesson comes from the Lord of heaven's armies. He gives wonderful advice. He is very wise.

Isaiah 28:29

A counsellor is a person who is trained to give guidance and advice. Usually, people go to counsellors when they want help with solving a problem, or to understand their emotions.

When we are faced with a decision or problem, we may ask friends for help, or we might see a professional counsellor. Asking those we trust for advice can be a good way to work through situations.

Many people offer advice, but God gives the BEST advice. The Bible says God gives 'wonderful advice' and is 'very wise'! The God who commands heaven's armies is our wise and compassionate counsellor – guiding us through life.

QUESTION TIME!

Who is the wisest person you know? Have you ever asked them for advice?

What is the best advice you've ever been given?

How does God counsel us? Why is it good to ask God for counsel?

Can you think of any advice God gives us in the Bible?

LET'S PRAY . . .

Dear God, thank you for offering me the best advice in the whole world through the Bible. I trust you to guide me with your wonderful wisdom.
Amen.

63

I AM YOUR AUTHORITY

Then Jesus came to them and said, 'All power in heaven and on earth is given to me.'

Matthew 28:18

You might hear the word 'authority' when someone talks about the government, police officers, or even your teachers. Authority means having power to make rules AND make sure people follow them!

Jesus tells us that ALL power in heaven and earth has been given to him, which means he has the authority over people, feelings, evil, sickness. Everything!

Jesus shares his authority with us too. We use his authority when we pray for healing, speak words of hope to others who are discouraged or worried, and fight evil, all in Jesus' name!

QUESTION TIME!

Have you ever wanted to be a police officer, teacher, or government worker?

Jesus has all the power in the world! Why has all the authority been given to Jesus?

Why do we have power when we pray and do things in Jesus' name?

Can you think of anything Jesus would like us to do, using his name and power?

LET'S PRAY . . .

Dear God, all authority in heaven and on earth is yours! Help me use the authority you give me to bring about good in your name.
Amen.

64

I AM YOUR BREATH OF LIFE

Then the Lord God took dust from the ground and formed man from it. The Lord breathed the breath of life into the man's nose. And the man became a living person.

Genesis 2:7

Do you ever think about breathing? It's something we usually forget about – even though we do it all day long! Breathing keeps us alive.

When God created the world, he created humans from the dust on the ground. Does dust breathe? No! So, God breathed the breath of life into humans. This is why we have breath, this is why we are alive.

Every time we breathe, it is a reminder that God is our breath of life, and because of him we have life!

QUESTION TIME!

Have you ever had to hold your breath for a long time? How did it make you feel?

What do we use our breath for? (Singing, whistling, speaking, shouting, living)

Where did our breath come from?

How can we use our breath to praise God?

LET'S PRAY . . .

Dear God, thank you for being my breath of life. Help me to use every breath I have to praise you and say good things!
Amen.

65 I AM YOUR INSPIRATION

Through his power all things were made – things in heaven and on earth, things seen and unseen, all powers, authorities, lords, and rulers. All things were made through Christ and for Christ.

Colossians 1:16

Look around. What inspires you? Is it nature, the people you see, or maybe the mysteries of time and space? Whether visible or invisible, everything was made by God!

So, God is the creator of EVERYTHING, which means creativity begins and ends with him! In him and his creation we find inspiration. God made us to discover his universe, to see beauty in each other and to find joy in our surroundings.

When we make artwork, build things, or even experiment in the kitchen, we are imitating God's love for creation and finding inspiration in the world he made. Our Creator loves inspiring us to create!

QUESTION TIME!

What is inspiration?

What inspires you?

Why is God the most creative being that exists?

How can you use your inspiration to glorify God?

LET'S PRAY . . .

Dear God, everything you've created is amazing. Thank you for giving me all the inspiration I need to be creative too!

Amen.

I AM YOUR SHOULDER TO CRY ON

Turn to me and be kind to me. I am lonely and hurting.

Psalm 25:16

If any of us has ever felt so sad we wanted to cry, the Bible has good news for us.

God knows when we're sad. He says he is close to us when we are hurting. He wants to be the shoulder we cry on, and the one we turn to when we feel all alone.

God isn't just close to us when we're sad, he also comforts us when we feel broken. He gives us strength when we don't feel we have any strength left.

QUESTION TIME!

Have you ever felt really sad?

How does God help you when you're sad?

Can you think of a time you felt comforted by God?

How can you cry on God's shoulder when you have a broken heart?

LET'S PRAY . . .

Dear God, sometimes I feel sad and want to cry. Help me remember that when I feel this way, you are close to me and ready to give me strength. ***Amen.***

I AM YOUR SAFE PLACE

The everlasting God is your place of safety.
His arms will hold you up forever.

Deuteronomy 33:27a

A lot of us have a favourite place – somewhere we like to be more than any other place. It could be a room in our house, or even at the park! Spending time in our favourite place can make us feel happy and safe.

As we imagine our favourite place, let's imagine God wrapping his arms around us in that place – holding us. The Bible tells us that God is our place a safety, and he will wrap his arms around us forever.

We can't see God like we can see our favourite place, but he is still with us and all around us. God is our place of safety, a place we can enjoy and feel comforted.

QUESTION TIME!

What is your favourite place?

How does spending time in your favourite place make you feel?

What does God say is a safe space for us?

In what ways does God wrap his arms around you?

LET'S PRAY . . .

Dear God, help me to remember that you are my place of safety. Thank you that you always have your arms around me, offering me peace and comfort.
Amen.

I AM YOUR TREASURE

Not only those things, but I think that all things are worth nothing compared with the greatness of knowing Christ Jesus my Lord. Because of Christ, I have lost all those things. And now I know that all those things are worthless trash. This allows me to have Christ.

Philippians 3:8

The apostle Paul writes that he would rather lose everything than lose Jesus because he considers all things 'worthless trash' compared to knowing Jesus!

It's easy to think of our favourite possessions that we would never throw away – for example, our books, our snacks, or our electronic devices. What Paul wants us to consider is that no matter how important those favourite things are to us, Jesus is even BETTER!

Jesus is our treasure and when we find him, he offers us joy, love, forgiveness and grace – that is, his unearned favour! Jesus makes us happier than all our favourite things combined ever could!

QUESTION TIME!

What is the most valuable thing you own?

Why is Jesus our treasure?

How can we show Jesus he is more valuable than our favourite possessions?

How can we get to know Jesus, our treasure, more every day?

LET'S PRAY . . .

Dear God, you are more valuable than anything in this world, even the most valuable treasures. Thank you for making yourself available to me.
Amen.

I AM YOUR JUSTICE

The Lord does what is right and fair,
for all who are wronged by others.

Psalm 103:6

When someone receives justice, it means they receive fair treatment for their actions. For example, if a student doesn't turn in their homework, then the fair treatment for their action is they fail the assignment.

God is full of mercy and forgiveness, and he also loves justice and doing what is fair. God cares very much about doing what is right for people who have been treated unfairly by others.

At times we might not think we receive fair treatment. Maybe a person who hurt us got away with it and wasn't punished. It doesn't seem fair! In these moments, when we don't see justice, we can call on God for justice. He will do what is right and fair in his perfect timing.

QUESTION TIME!

Can you think of an example of justice?

Can you think of a time you felt something was unfair?

When something hurtful happens to you, how can you trust God to do what is fair?

In what ways can you love justice like God loves justice?

LET'S PRAY . . .

Dear God, I will trust you to do what is fair. Help me to believe you will do what is right when I have been wronged. ***Amen.***

I AM YOUR MEDIATOR

There is only one God. And there is only one way that people can reach God. That way is through Jesus Christ, who is also a man.

1 Timothy 2:5

A mediator is someone who helps fix a problem between two people. The mediator works to find a solution to the problem in order to help bring peace!

When Adam and Eve disobeyed God in the Garden of Eden, a problem formed between people and God. Their disobedience didn't match God's perfect plan.

To fix the problem, Jesus became our mediator. He stands between God and people to bring peace. Jesus is the reason we can have a loving relationship with God!

QUESTION TIME!

Have you ever needed someone's help to resolve a problem between you and a friend?

Have you ever helped solve a problem between two friends?

Why do you need a mediator to have a relationship with God?

Why is Jesus the perfect mediator between you and God?

LET'S PRAY . . .

Dear God, thank you for sending Jesus to be my mediator so I can have a relationship with you. Thank you for your love and patience!

Amen.

I AM YOUR JOY

Shout and sing for joy, you people of Jerusalem.
The Holy One of Israel does great things before your eyes.

Isaiah 12:6

Sometimes we feel like shouting and singing because something great has happened and we can't hold our happiness inside!

The writer of Isaiah told the people of Jerusalem to 'sing for joy' because of all the great things God, the Holy One of Israel, was doing. Well, God is STILL doing lots of great things today!

Whether life is going well or life is tough, we can find overwhelming joy in how GREAT God is. We can look around at all the amazing things God's doing and find joy in how wonderful he is.

QUESTION TIME!

What things make you feel joyful?

What do you do when you're feeling happy or joyful?

How can we find joy in God?

Can you name a few amazing things God does every day?

LET'S PRAY . . .
Dear God, thank you for giving me so many reasons to be joyful! All I need to do is look around to see the great things you're doing.
Amen.

I AM YOUR GUARDIAN

The Lord will guard you as you come and go,
both now and forever.

Psalm 121:8

Have you ever seen a guard? Maybe they were guarding a bank, a shop, or even a palace where a royal family lives. Only places and things that are valuable need a guard.

Guards watch every person passing by, very closely. If anything or anyone threatens the safety of what they guard, they are ready to jump into action and defend it!

God is our guardian. He watches over us as we go about our lives. God is always paying attention to the things happening around us and to us. He is ready to jump into action when we need help.

QUESTION TIME!

Have you ever seen a guard? What were they guarding?

In what ways is God like a guard?

Why does God guard you?

What kinds of things does God guard you from?

LET'S PRAY . . .

Dear God, thank you for guarding me day and night. You see everything and are ready to help me when I need it. ***Amen.***

73

I AM YOUR GOOD NEWS

For God loved the world so much that he gave his only Son. God gave his Son so that whoever believes in him may not be lost but have eternal life.

John 3:16

When we see people reading the news in a newspaper, on their phone, or watching the TV, we might wonder whether the news they're reading is good or bad.

No matter what the TV says, we always have good news! Why? Because God loved us so much that he sent his Son, Jesus, to save us. Now, anyone who believes in Jesus has eternal life.

The best part of this good news is that it is for EVERYONE! When we share the good news, we share the love and hope God gives us.

QUESTION TIME!

What is the best news you've ever heard? How did it make you feel?

Why do we need good news?

Have you ever shared the good news of Jesus with anyone?

How can we share the good news with the world?

LET'S PRAY . . .

Dear God, you are my good news! Thank you for sending Jesus to offer eternal life to everyone. Make me a messenger of that good news.

Amen.

I AM YOUR EQUIPPER

Using the Scriptures, the person who serves God will be ready and will have everything he needs to do every good work.

2 Timothy 3:17

What does it mean when someone is equipped? A person who is equipped has what they need to get a job done.

Here's an example: to brush your teeth, you need to be equipped with a toothbrush, toothpaste and water, or else the job will be impossible!

When God asks us to do something, he also has the equipment we need to get the job done. Even if we feel unprepared for what God is asking us to do, we can trust him.

QUESTION TIME!

Can you think of a job you would need to be equipped to do?

Why can you trust God to equip you for good works?

How does God give you what you need to serve him?

Can you think of something God has asked you to do?

LET'S PRAY . . .

Dear God, there are times I feel unable or afraid to do what you want me to do. When I feel like this, please remind me that you will equip me and give me what I need.

Amen.

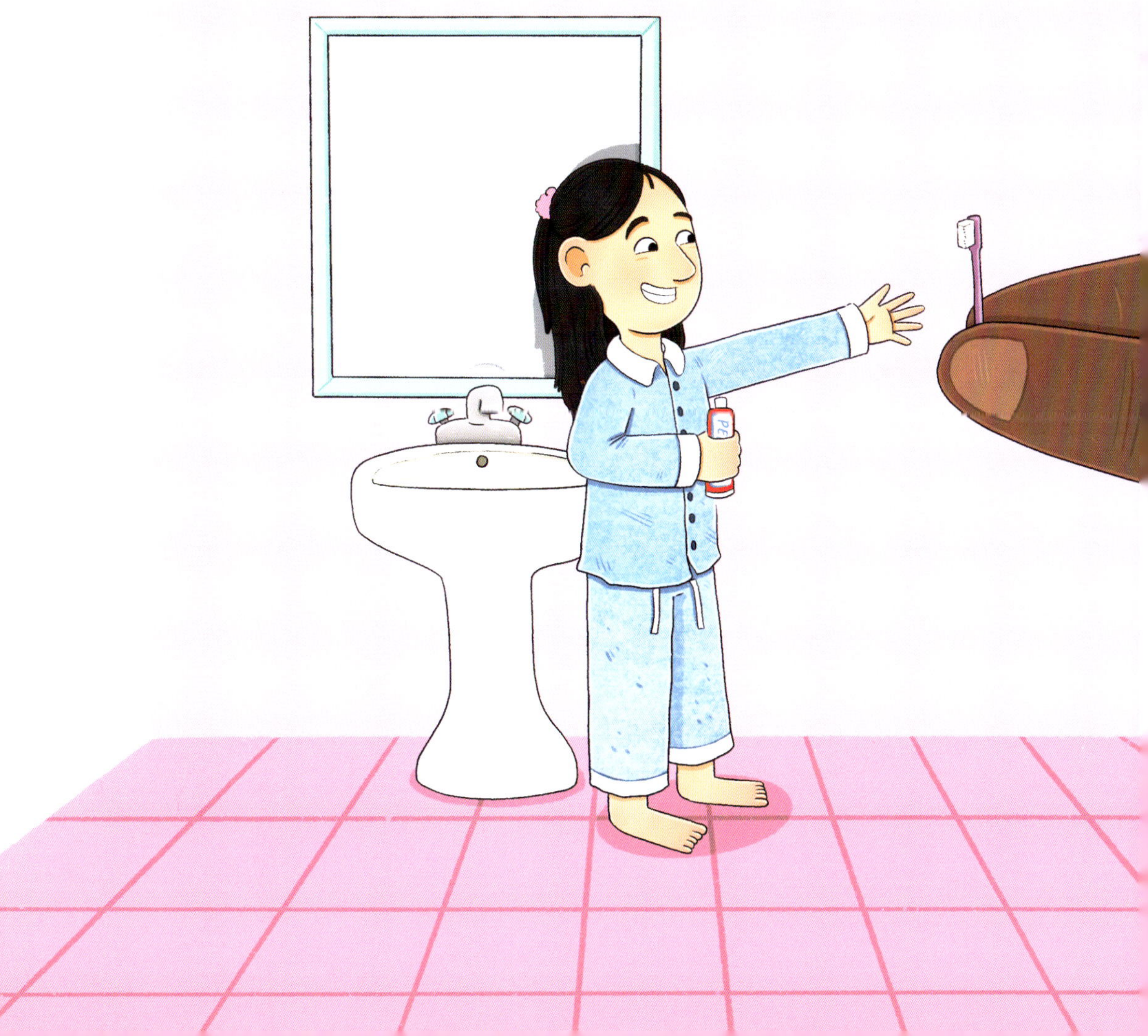

I AM YOUR CAPTAIN

Patience and encouragement come from God. And I pray that God will help you all agree with each other the way Christ Jesus wants. Then you will all be joined together, and you will give glory to God the Father of our Lord Jesus Christ.

Romans 15:5–6

The captain of a team is responsible for uniting their teammates. A good captain encourages their team to work together towards a shared goal – usually to win a game!

God is our captain, and he is encouraging his team, Christians all over the world, towards a shared goal. The goal is that Jesus would be glorified, and the world would know his love.

When we spend time arguing with one another, we are not acting like we're on the same team. But when we join together in Jesus' name, as one team, we bring glory to God AND show God's love to the world!

QUESTION TIME!

What should a team do to work together well?

How is God like the captain of a team?

Who is on God's team? Why is it important the church works as a team?

Why does God want the church/Christians to join together?

LET'S PRAY . . .

Dear God, help me be united with other Christians to bring you glory. You are my captain, and I know you want what's best for me and for your church.
Amen.

76

I AM YOUR COMPANION

The Lord himself will go before you. He will be with you. He will not leave you or forget you. Don't be afraid. Don't worry.

Deuteronomy 31:8

A companion is someone who goes with another person wherever they go. God is our companion, because he never leaves us or forgets about us.

Although we can't see or hear God in the same way we can see our friends and family, he is still right beside us. He sees and hears us, he listens and laughs, he cries with us and comforts us.

There will never be someone as close to us who knows us better than God does.

QUESTION TIME!

Can you think of a friend or family member who is a good companion?

What are some good things about God being our companion?

How can you spend time with God when you can't physically see or audibly hear him?

How does it make you feel that God goes everywhere with you?

LET'S PRAY . . .

Dear God, thank you that you are always with me and will never forget me. When I feel alone, help me to remember you're with me.
Amen.

I AM YOUR HOME

We know that our body – the tent we live in here on earth – will be destroyed. But when that happens, God will have a house for us to live in. It will not be a house made by men. It will be a home in heaven that will last forever.

2 Corinthians 5:1

When we think of home, we might think of the place we live with our family. We cook meals, decorate our bedrooms, have friends over and spend a lot of time in our homes.

To 'feel at home' means to feel like you belong. On earth we have a physical home, where we live, but we don't belong on earth forever. The Bible tells us we have a home in heaven, made by God himself!

Our true home is with God in heaven, where we belong – sharing forever with our heavenly Father.

QUESTION TIME!

What do you enjoy or dislike about being at home?

Where do you 'feel at home' or feel like you belong?

What do you think your home is like in heaven?

Why is it good to remember our home in heaven while we're on earth?

LET'S PRAY . . .

Dear God, thank you for preparing a home for me in heaven. I praise you for giving me a place I will belong and be welcomed forever.

Amen.

78

I AM YOUR VOICE OF TRUTH

So Jesus said to the Jews who believed in him, 'If you continue to obey my teaching, you are truly my followers. Then you will know the truth. And the truth will make you free.'

John 8:31–32

The Bible is called the 'Word of God', and it teaches us. As we read it, we hear God's voice through the words. When we obey and follow Jesus, we will know the truth and it will set us free.

If we believe the truth, Jesus says we WILL be free! Look at these examples of truth from the Bible and how they set us free:

1. God says he has good plans for our lives.

   We are set free from worrying that our lives don't have meaning.

2. God says we are loved, valuable, and made in his image.

   We are set free from feeling worthless and ugly.

3. God says he will never leave us or forsake us.

   We are set free from loneliness and exclusion.

QUESTION TIME!

How does the truth change our lives?

Why is it important we believe the truth and not lies?

How can the truth set us free?

Can you give an example of truth from the Bible?

LET'S PRAY . . .

*Dear God, you speak the truth,
and the truth sets me free!
Thank you for speaking through
the Bible so that I can be free.*
Amen.

79

I AM YOUR POWER

But the Lord said to me, 'My grace is enough for you. When you are weak, then my power is made perfect in you.' So I am very happy to brag about my weaknesses. Then Christ's power can live in me.

2 Corinthians 12:9

Many people think power is found in strength, but God says HIS power is made perfect in our weakness! That means when we are weak, God replaces our weakness with HIS strength and power.

Because of God's grace, we can admit our weaknesses without feeling ashamed. In fact, we can tell everyone about our weaknesses because we know that God will make us strong.

So, we don't need to hide our weaknesses from other people or be afraid to ask for help. Instead, we can let people see God's strength, grace and power in us.

QUESTION TIME!

What is weakness?

Have you ever wanted to hide your weakness from your friends or family?

How does God give you his power and strength when you're weak?

Why do we need God's power in our weakness?

LET'S PRAY . . .

Dear God, I am glad that weakness isn't something I should hide, because when I am weak you give me your power! Thank you for making me strong.

Amen.

I AM YOUR POTTER

But Lord, you are our father.
We are like clay, and you are the potter.
Your hands made us all.

Isaiah 64:8

A potter is someone who uses clay to create various ordinary pots and artistic pieces. The potter begins by moulding the clay with his hands as it spins on a wheel. Some pieces are tall and thin, while others are smooth and curved. Each piece is different and unique.

The potter decides what a pot will look like and what it will be used for. Our potter, God, also decides what we look like and how he will use us.

God carefully moulds each of us according to what he knows is best. Every person is a work of art, created and designed with purpose by God. We are all unique.

QUESTION TIME!

Can you think of a time you compared your appearance and purpose to someone else?

Why is it unhelpful to compare yourself to others?

Do you ever wonder why God has made you the way you are?

How can you practise loving God's design and unique purpose for your life?

LET'S PRAY . . .

Dear God, thank you for making me the way I am on purpose! Please show me how you'd like to use me. ***Amen.***

81 I AM YOUR VINE

I am the vine, and you are the branches. If a person remains in me and I remain in him, then he produces much fruit. But without me he can do nothing.

John 15:5

A vine is a type of plant that grows along a wall or across a fence, for example, a grapevine. The branches attached to the vine produce a lot of grapes! But a branch that gets disconnected eventually withers and dies.

The Bible uses the example of a vine and branches to symbolise our connection to God. If we are attached to God, following and putting him first in our lives, then we will produce fruit – good things like love, joy, peace and patience! But, if we aren't connected to God, we won't produce good fruits.

Just like a vine is the source of life for all its branches, God is the source of life for Christians. People who stay connected to God will live lives that produce many good fruits.

QUESTION TIME!

Can you name some good fruit – physical and spiritual?

How do we stay connected to God, our source of life?

How can we become disconnected from God?

Why can't we produce good fruit apart from God?

LET'S PRAY . . .

Dear God, you are my source of life and in you, I produce good fruit. Help me to stay actively connected to you so that good things like love, joy and peace are produced in me.

Amen.

I AM YOUR ARMOUR

Finally, be strong in the Lord and in his great power. Wear the full armour of God. Wear God's armour so that you can fight against the devil's evil tricks.

Ephesians 6:10–11

Every superhero puts on their super suit before they fight a villain! The armour of God is the suit we put on to defend ourselves against the devil's tricks.

The devil lies to us constantly, trying to convince us that God doesn't truly love us and we don't belong in God's family. We might be tempted to believe the lies, but God has given us a full set of armour to defend ourselves and fight back.

The armour of God protects us and gives us strength. It's important we put it on every day by reading God's Word and trusting him. We never know when we'll need to defend ourselves!

QUESTION TIME!

Are you good at recognising when someone is lying?

Can you name a lie the devil tries to use against you?

Why do you need to put on God's armour?

How will putting on the armour of God help you today?

LET'S PRAY . . .

Dear God, thank you for being my armour so I can fight against the devil's lies. Help me to remember to put on your armour every day! ***Amen.***

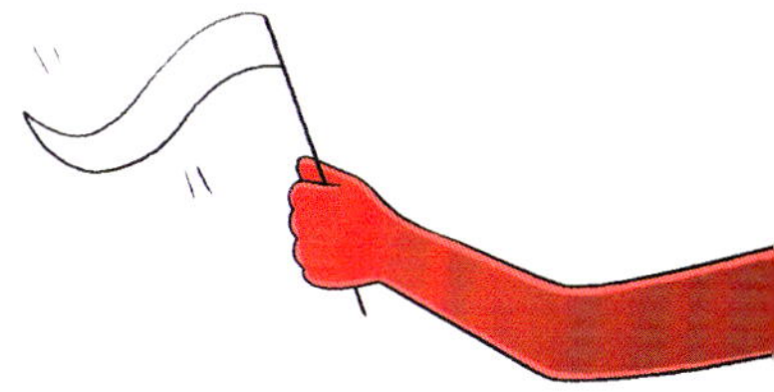

I AM YOUR BREAD

Then Jesus said, 'I am the bread that gives life.
He who comes to me will never be hungry.
He who believes in me will never be thirsty.'

John 6:35

We have physical bodies which we can see, and we have souls which we can't see. Our bodies need food to stay alive and our souls need Jesus to be alive. This is why Jesus compares himself to bread – he is the food for our soul.

Food gives our bodies energy to play sports, spend time with friends and do activities – eating food gives us life. Jesus, our bread, gives us a different kind of life – he gives us eternal life!

Anyone who eats bread will have physical life, but anyone who hears about Jesus and believes in him will have eternal life.

QUESTION TIME!

Have you ever gone a long time without eating? How did it make you feel?

In what ways is Jesus like bread?

How does Jesus feed your soul?

Where can we find energy to follow God and do his will?

LET'S PRAY . . .

Dear God, thank you for giving my spirit energy and for keeping me alive! Without you, I would not have eternal life.

Amen.

I AM YOUR AVENGER

My friends, do not try to punish others when they wrong you. Wait for God to punish them with his anger. It is written: 'I am the One who punishes; I will pay people back,' says the Lord.

Romans 12:19

An avenger is a person who inflicts punishment in return for an injury or wrong done to someone else.

God doesn't turn away when people hurt us. He sees what happens and he promises to avenge us by bringing fair punishment. God will take care of defending us.

It may be tempting to take revenge, especially if we feel hurt and angry. Instead, we can trust God and the promises he makes. He will avenge us and bring punishment in his timing.

QUESTION TIME!

Can you think of a time you wanted to take revenge? What did you do?

How can you resist the temptation to take revenge?

Why can you trust God to avenge you?

Why is it better to let God avenge you than for you to take revenge on someone?

LET'S PRAY . . .

Dear God, sometimes I want to hurt the people who've hurt me. It's hard to trust you to take care of it, but I know you will avenge me. Help me to be patient.

Amen.

I AM YOUR SECOND CHANCE

The Lord shows mercy and is kind. He does not become angry quickly, and he has great love.

Psalm 103:8

Have you ever tried to hit the centre of a target with a bow and arrow? It's difficult! If you miss the target the first time, you probably want to keep trying until you get a bullseye.

The target represents what pleases God. When we sin, we miss the target by not obeying him. God could get angry and refuse to forgive us, but he doesn't! He is merciful and kind, does not get angry quickly and is overflowing with love.

God gives us a second chance when we mess up! When God gives us second chances, we should not take advantage of his kindness by continuing to sin. Instead, his mercy and love should cause us to obey and adore him more.

QUESTION TIME!

Have you ever messed up when doing something and wanted a second chance?

When have you received a second chance?

How does God respond to you when you sin/mess up?

How should you respond to God when he gives you second chances?

LET'S PRAY . . .

Dear God, thank you for forgiving me. Your mercy and love for me means that I don't have to be afraid of messing up. Help me to use every second chance to obey you more. ***Amen.***

I AM YOUR RESCUER

God made us free from the power of darkness, and he brought us into the kingdom of his dear Son.

Colossians 1:13

To rescue someone means to save them from experiencing something negative, like pain or embarrassment.

As humans, we were born with a sinful nature – a desire to disobey God. As much as we try to obey and love God, we can't help but mess up sometimes. Our sinful nature can cause us to feel trapped in bad decisions and feel full of guilt and shame.

This is why we need someone to rescue us. We need God to remind us that he set us FREE from our sinful nature. God brought us out of darkness and showed us the kingdom of his Son, Jesus!

QUESTION TIME!

Have you ever been rescued from a dangerous situation?

Have you ever rescued something or someone?

Why do we need to be rescued? And how?

What does it mean for God to bring us out of darkness and into the kingdom of Jesus?

LET'S PRAY . . .

Dear God, thank you for rescuing me from sin and shame. When I feel trapped by bad decisions and negative feelings, you remind me that I am free!
Amen.

I AM YOUR TEACHER

Accept my work and learn from me. I am gentle and humble in spirit. And you will find rest for your souls.

Matthew 11:29

An effective teacher demonstrates what they know to their students. Jesus is an expert in rest, humility and gentleness. He encourages us to learn from him as our teacher.

If we learn from Jesus and do what he does, we will find rest from the chaos around us. And if we continue to watch him, take notes and practise what he does, we will become more like him in every part of our lives.

Only Jesus can teach us the best way to live our lives, because he lived a perfect life!

QUESTION TIME!

Can you think of a time someone taught you how to do something?

What things have you learned from Jesus? How does he teach you?

Why is Jesus the best person to teach you how to live?

What can you do to be a good student of Jesus?

LET'S PRAY . . .

Dear God, thank you for teaching me how to live the best life I can live. Help me to keep learning from you every day.
Amen.

I AM YOUR ALLY

Yes, God is working in you to help you want to do what pleases him. Then he gives you the power to do it.

Philippians 2:13

An ally is a person who partners with someone else to help them.

God is our ally because he helps us do what pleases him. God works in our hearts to WANT good things, then he gives us power to DO good things. Without God's help and his alliance, we would not naturally choose to do what pleases him!

If we want to do what pleases God, we can be confident that God will help us every step of the way. He is our ally and will work in us and with us.

QUESTION TIME!

What is the importance of having an ally?

Have you ever been helped by an ally?

What kinds of things does God help you do?

Why do we need God's help to do good things?

LET'S PRAY . . .

Dear God, thank you for teaming up with me so I can do things that please you. Please give me the desire to do good things.
Amen.

89

I AM YOUR BEGINNING AND END

I am the Alpha and the Omega, the First and the Last, the Beginning and the End.

Revelation 22:13

We all have a beginning and end on earth (when we are born and when we die), but God does not. God stands outside of time. He existed before the world was created, and he will continue to exist forever!

God created everything – he gave the universe it's beginning, and he will be there to the very end. He has been present for every minute of history and he will be present for every minute of our lives.

Our friends, family and things come and go, but God is with us forever, from beginning to end.

QUESTION TIME!

Are you waiting for something to start or end?

Have you ever wished something would never end? What was it?

How do you feel when you hear that God stands outside of time?

Why is it comforting to know God is our beginning to end?

LET'S PRAY . . .

Dear God, you are my beginning and end! Thank you for writing my story and being with me every step along the way. ***Amen.***

90

I AM YOUR PEACE

I told you these things so that you can have peace in me.
In this world you will have trouble. But be brave!
I have defeated the world!

John 16:33

Imagine sitting in a park on a sunny day. Everything is peaceful. And then, a stampede of elephants runs right through the park! The park doesn't seem very peaceful anymore, does it?

When we feel like we're out of control, it's like we're in a park full of elephants. But Jesus tells us that even when we feel that way, we can still have peace in our hearts.

Every person experiences trouble in their life which they don't have control over. No one can avoid it. But thanks to Jesus, we can be brave and have peace, because we know he is in control. Jesus has defeated our troubles!

QUESTION TIME!

Can you describe what peace feels like to you?

Can you describe a time when you felt out of control?

How can you be brave in times when you don't feel peace?

How can you find peace in Jesus?

LET'S PRAY . . .

Dear God, thank you that when I have troubles, I can trust you are in control of this world. Help me to find my peace in you and not the things around me.
Amen.

CONCLUSION

I AM WHO I AM

Then God said to Moses, 'I AM WHO I AM. When you go to the people of Israel, tell them, "I AM sent me to you."'

Exodus 3:14

We can't put God in a box, or define him. God is mysterious, we will never understand him completely or know everything about him. We see pieces of him and who he is, but he is so much bigger, better and more wonderful than we can even imagine.

One thing is certain, there is no one like God. He is the only God in the universe and he does not depend on anyone or anything. God existed before the beginning of time and will continue to exist forever. He has no beginning and no end.

Even though we will never know everything about God, because he is infinite, he invites us into a loving, personal relationship with himself. Can you believe such a big God would reveal himself to us and promise to love us forever?

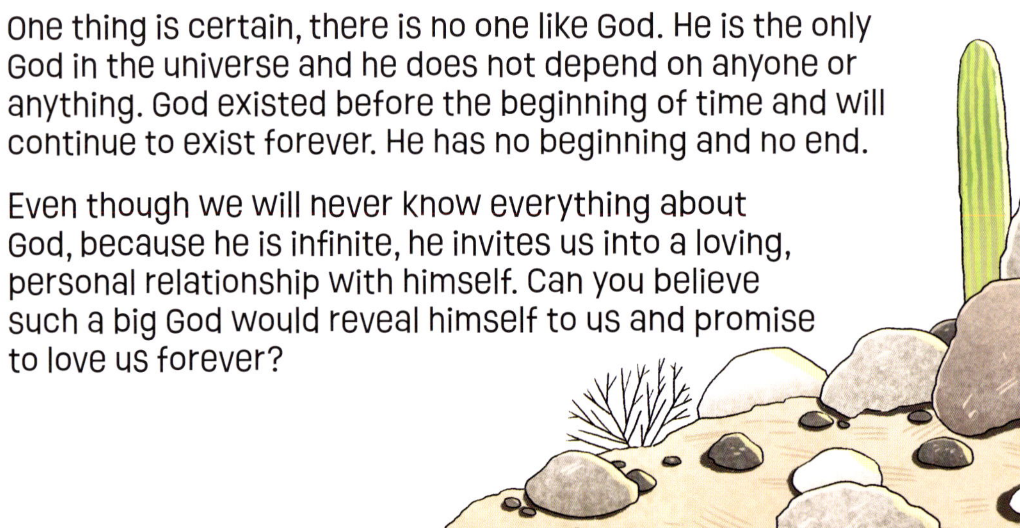

Dear God, you are amazing, mysterious, and infinite – I can't even wrap my mind around all that you are. Thank you for loving me and wanting a friendship with me. I want to keep getting to know you forever!

Amen.

THE LORD'S PRAYER

Jesus said to them, "When you pray, say:

'Father, we pray that your name will always be kept holy.
We pray that your kingdom will come.
Give us the food we need for each day.
Forgive us the sins we have done,
because we forgive every person who has done wrong to us.
And do not cause us to be tested.'"

Amen
Luke 11: 2-4

MY NOTES

MY NOTES

MY NOTES

Do you want to read more of the Bible?

Then get your copy of *The International Children's Bible!*

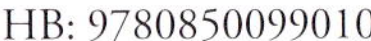
HB: 9780850099010

HB: 9781860244315

PB: 9781788931465

The *International Children's Bible* is not an adult Bible especially packaged for children. It has specifically been translated directly from the Hebrew and Greek texts into English so that it can be read and understood by children between the ages of 6 and 12.

The *ICB* is a full text Bible that every child will be delighted to own. With guidance, daily Bible reading can easily become a pleasurable habit that will last a lifetime.

Features of the full *ICB* include:

- Large, easy to read type in two columns
- Simple footnotes explain names, customs and phrases
- 32 full colour illustrations with multicultural images
- A dictionary helps explains difficult words and phrases
- Presentation page
- Colour maps
- Ribbon marker

With simpler language and extra notes and helps, the *ICB* is the perfect Bible for a child who is ready to move on from a picture Bible to a full text Bible.